Knitted Toy Travels

Ed the Explorer packs up his case.
He jumps on a plane with a smile on his face.

There are so many creatures he can't wait to spy,
From the long-necked giraffe to parrots that fly.

There are hippos and zebras and tigers that roar,
Kangaroos, meerkats and so many more.

Ed the Explorer jumps off the plane
And dreams of a great lion shaking his mane.

Knitted Toy Travels

15 wild knitting projects from across the globe

LAURA LONG

David and Charles

www.rucraft.co.uk

Contents

Introduction

We all have memories of wonderful holidays and exciting places we have visited. I have particularly fond and exciting memories of visiting London Zoo when I was young. While walking around the zoo I created little stories about the different animals and imagined what their lives were like and which other creatures they were friends with.

This collection of sweet little knitted animals brings out the child in all of us. Creating beautiful toys out of yarn can remind you of special places and creatures, and can be enjoyed for many years to come.

Each toy animal in this book has its own unique character and all the animals are linked by Explorer Ed's travels around the world. In every country he visits, he meets a new animal, each with a different story to tell.

There are projects in this book for everyone to enjoy knitting, from beginners to more advanced knitters. If you are a beginner, I would advise you to start with a simple project that is small, easy and quick to knit. There is nothing more satisfying than knitting a finished piece in an hour or two. Once you have mastered the techniques you can move on to make any animal. Don't be scared, I promise that there isn't a single animal that is too hard to knit!

I am not a fan of knitting lots of components and then sewing them together afterwards. I like to see a toy develop as it is being knitted. So, I have developed all the patterns with shaping that creates three-dimensional shapes. The different parts and colours are introduced while you knit.

Knitting is fun and for everyone.

Ed the Explorer

Rating ✈ to ✈ ✈ ✈

See individual project patterns for more detail

One day Edward decided he wanted to explore the world. He packed his map, his compass, some warm clothes and some cool clothes and set off on his journey from country to country. He also packed a pen and some paper so he could tick off which countries he had visited and make notes about the animals he met along the way. Ed is a very friendly explorer. He likes to meet new animals and make everyone laugh with his silly jokes.

There are various elements to this project. First come the instructions for making Ed the Explorer himself, including his hair. Then there are patterns for his two outfits. His warm-weather shorts and jacket are accompanied by an adorable hat, socks, boots, a belt and a handy bag. The patterns for his winter gear include a coat, woolly hat and mittens.

Yarn
Lightweight (DK) yarn:
1 x 1¾oz (50g) ball in pale pink (MC)
Oddments for hair and facial features

Needles
Size 6 (4mm) knitting needles

Gauge
22 sts and 30 rows to 4in (10cm)

Finished size
17½in (44cm) tall

Ed the Explorer has got itchy feet.
He walks through the desert
not minding the heat.

Exploring the mountains,
the jungles and snow,

There isn't a landscape
where Ed will not go.

Ed the Explorer pattern

HEAD, BODY AND LEGS

Starting at top of head, cast on 7 sts in **yarn MC** using size 6 (4mm) knitting needles.

Row 1 [Kfb] 6 times, k1. (13 sts)
Row 2 P.
Row 3 [Kfb, k1, kfb] 4 times, k1. (21 sts)
Row 4 P.
Row 5 [Kfb, k3, kfb] 4 times, k1. (29 sts)
Row 6 P.
Row 7 [Kfb, k5, kfb] 4 times, k1. (37 sts)
Row 8 P.
Row 9 K8, kfb, kfb, k16, kfb, kfb, k9. (41 sts)
Cont in st st for 15 rows.
Row 25 K8, skpo, k2tog, k16, skpo, k2tog, k9. (37 sts)
Row 26 P.
Row 27 [K2tog, k5, skpo] 4 times, k1. (29 sts)
Row 28 P.
Row 29 K.
Row 30 P.

Cont for the body:
Row 31 [Kfb] rep to end. (58 sts)
Row 32 P.
Cont in st st for 30 rows.
Row 63 [K2tog] rep to end. (29 sts)

Cont for the legs:
Row 64 P14, p2tog, p13 (hold first 14 sts for left leg on stitch holder and cont on 14 sts for right leg).
Cont in st st for 50 rows.

Cont for the feet:
Row 115 K6, kfb, kfb, k6. (16 sts)
Row 116 P.
Row 117 K7, kfb, kfb, k7. (18 sts)
Row 118 P.
Row 119 K8, kfb, kfb, k8. (20 sts)
Row 120 P2tog, p16, p2tog. (18 sts)
Row 121 K2tog, k14, k2tog. (16 sts)
Row 122 [P2tog] rep to end. (8 sts)
Thread yarn through rem sts and pull tight.
Rep on rem 14 sts for left leg.

ARMS (MAKE 2)

Cast on 14 sts in **yarn MC** using size 6 (4mm) knitting needles. St st for 40 rows.
Row 41 [K2tog] rep to end. (7 sts)
Thread yarn through rem sts and pull tight.

MAKING UP

BODY
The head, body and legs are knitted all as one piece.
Sew down the back of the head and body and fill with stuffing (see Techniques: Making up).
Sew down the back of the legs to the tips of the toes. Because the legs are thin it is easier to fill them with stuffing as you go.

KNEES
Halfway down the leg, pinch a couple of rows of stitches together, and stitch in place using **yarn MC**. This will give Ed knobbly knees and that extra bit of character! Sew the yarn neatly inside the leg so that no ends are showing.

ARMS
Sew up the arm seams, filling with stuffing as you go. Sew the arms onto the body using the shaping at the neck to help with positioning.

HAIR
Thread up two strands of brown yarn (or blond, ginger or black, depending on the colour of hair you want). Stitch around the head to create the basic shape of the hair. Start at the fringe and work your way around the back.
Fill in the hair area with flat stitches about ⅜in (1cm) long – it can take some time!

FACIAL FEATURES
Embroider the eyes using brown or black yarn (see Techniques: Embroidering details).
Pinch two stitches together just below the centre of the eyes and stitch in place using **yarn MC** (just like the knees, but much smaller). This creates the nose. Sew the yarn neatly inside the body so that no ends are showing. Using dark pink or red yarn, make two or three stitches just below the nose to create the mouth.

11

Ed's warm-weather clothing

Rating 🛩🛩

The jacket is the hardest item to make here. The other pieces are fairly simple, but there are a lot of them!

Edward knew that on his travels he would be visiting countries that were very hot like Australia and Africa. He also knew that he would need to have some lightweight clothes for these places, like these shorts and matching jacket. You can change the colour of the clothes to give Edward a whole new wardrobe. And you can lengthen the shorts to make the trousers for when he explores the Arctic.

Yarn
Lightweight (DK) yarn:
2 x 1¾oz (50g) balls in olive
green (**A**)
Oddment of white yarn (**B**)
Oddment of brown yarn (**C**)
Oddment of black yarn

Needles
Size 6 (4mm) knitting needles

Gauge
22 sts and 30 rows to 4in (10cm)

Finished sizes
To fit Ed

Warm-weather clothing patterns

SHORTS
Cast on 58 sts in **yarn A** using size 6 (4mm) knitting needles.
K1, p1 rib for 4 rows.
Cont in st st for 16 rows.

Cont for right leg:
Row 21 K29 turn.
Row 22 P29.
Cont in st st for 16 rows.
Row 39 K.
Row 40 K.
Row 41 K.
Row 42 K.
Bind off.
Rep for left leg.

POCKETS (MAKE 3)
Cast on 8 sts in **yarn A** using size 6 (4mm) knitting needles.
Row 1 K.
Row 2 K.
Row 3 K.
Row 4 P.
Cont in st st for 4 rows.
Bind off.

Rep to make two more pockets. One of the pockets will be used for Ed's jacket later on.

JACKET (MAKE 2)
Cast on 34 sts in **yarn A** using size 6 (4mm) knitting needles.
Knit 4 rows.
Cont in st st for 4 rows.
Row 9 K11, skpo, k8, k2tog, k11. (32 sts)
Row 10 P.
Cont in st st for 6 rows.
Row 17 K11, skpo, k6, k2tog, k11. (30 sts)
Row 18 P.
Cont in st st for 6 rows.
Row 25 K11, skpo, k4, k2tog, k11. (28 sts)
Row 26 P.
Cont in st st for 6 rows.

Cont for sleeves:
Row 33 Cast on 12 sts, k to end.
Row 34 Cast on 12 sts, p to end. (52 sts)
Cont in st st for 4 rows.
Row 39 K23, skpo, k2, k2tog, k23. (50 sts)
Row 40 P.
Cont in st st for 6 rows.
Row 47 K23, skpo, k2tog, k23. (48 sts)
Row 48 P.
Bind off.

HAT

Cast on 6 sts in **yarn A** using size 6 (4mm) knitting needles.

Row 1 [Kfb] 6 times. (12 sts)
Row 2 P.
Row 3 [Kfb] 12 times. (24 sts)
Row 4 P.
Row 5 [Kfb] 24 times. (48 sts)
Row 6 P.
Cont in st st for 10 rows.
Row 17 [Kfb, k10, kfb] 4 times. (56 sts)
Row 18 P.
Cont in st st for 2 rows.
Row 21 [Kfb, k12, kfb] 4 times. (64 sts)
Row 22 K.
Row 23 K.
Row 24 K.
Bind off.

SOCKS (MAKE 2)

Cast on 16 sts in **yarn B** using size 6 (4mm) knitting needles.

Row 1 K.
Row 2 K.
Row 3 K.
Row 4 K.
Cont in st st for 10 rows.
Row 15 K7, kfb, kfb, k7. (18 sts)
Row 16 P.
Row 17 K8, kfb, kfb, k8. (20 sts)
Row 18 P.
Row 19 K9, kfb, kfb, k9. (22 sts)
Row 20 P2tog, p18, p2tog. (20 sts)
Row 21 K2tog, k16, k2tog. (18 sts)
Row 22 [p2tog] rep to end. (9 sts)
Thread yarn through rem sts and pull tight.

BOOTS (MAKE 2)

Cast on 16 sts in **yarn C** using size 6 (4mm) knitting needles.

Row 1 K.
Row 2 K.
Row 3 K.
Row 4 P.
Row 5 K7, kfb, kfb, k7. (18 sts)
Row 6 P.
Row 7 K8, kfb, kfb, k8. (20 sts)
Row 8 P.
Row 9 K9, kfb, kfb, k9. (22 sts)
Row 10 P.
Row 11 K2tog, k18, k2tog. (20 sts)
Row 12 P2tog, p16, p2tog. (18 sts)
Row 13 [k2tog] rep to end. (9 sts)
Thread yarn through rem sts and pull tight.

BELT
Cast on 62 sts in **yarn C** using size 6 (4mm) knitting needles.
Knit 2 rows.
Bind off.

BAG
Cast on 12 sts in **yarn C** using size 6 (4mm) knitting needles.
St st for 11 rows.
Row 12 K to form a ridge.
Cont in st st for 13 rows.
Row 26 K to form a ridge.
Cont in st st for 6 rows.
Bind off.

BAG STRAP
Cast on 62 sts in **yarn C** using size 6 (4mm) knitting needles.
Knit 2 rows.
Bind off.

MAKING UP

SHORTS
Sew up the leg seams and down the back of the shorts (see Techniques: Making up).
Sew a pocket onto each leg of the shorts, making sure you position them at the same height on each side.

JACKET
Position the front of the jacket neatly on top of the back, right sides out.
Sew up the side seams, under the arms and along the shoulders, leaving a space for the neck.
Sew a pretend seam down the front of the jacket using black yarn.
Sew the pocket you made earlier onto the right-hand side of the jacket.

HAT, SOCKS AND BOOTS
Sew along the back seam of each item.

BELT
Sew on a popper to secure each end of the belt.

BAG
Fold the bag along the ridges and sew up the side seams.
Sew one end of the strap to each side of the bag.
Sew a popper onto the bag flap.

Ed's winter wear

Rating

*The warm coat is made of three separate pieces so
you need to assemble it accurately at the end*

Ed the Explorer has a warm winter coat for his travels to chilly places
like the Arctic. He also has a cosy hat and scarf. He even packed some
mittens so that his hands wouldn't get cold. Edward can be a bit clumsy
at times so he tied the mittens on elastic so he didn't loose them. You
certainly don't want to get cold hands in the Arctic! I used a thick, fluffy
yarn to make the warm winter coat and added poppers so that it can
removed easily. The hat and mittens use a much thinner yarn and could
be knitted in any colour you like. Be creative and make them as bright as
you can… After all, Ed the Explorer likes to make everyone laugh!

Yarn
Medium-weight (chunky)
merino yarn:
1 x 3½oz (100g) ball in soft
cream (**MC**)
Lightweight (DK) yarn:
Oddment of olive green (**A**)
Oddment of cream (**B**)

Needles
Size 10½ (7.5mm) knitting needles
Size 6 (4mm) knitting needles

Gauge
10 sts and 16 rows to 4in (10cm)

Finished sizes
To fit Ed

Winter-wear patterns

COAT BACK
Cast on 20 sts in **yarn MC** using size 10½ (7.5mm) knitting needles.
Knit 4 rows.
Cont in st st for 24 rows.
Sleeves:
Row 29 Cast on 10 sts, k to end.
Row 30 Cast on 10 sts, p to end. (40 sts)
Row 31 K14, skpo, k8, k2tog, k14. (38 sts)
Row 32 P.
Cont in st st for 8 rows.
Bind off.

COAT FRONTS (MAKE 2)
For left front, cast on 12 sts in **yarn MC** using size
10½ (7.5mm) knitting needles. .
Knit 4 rows.
Cont in st st for 24 rows.

Cont for sleeve:
Row 29 Cast on 10 sts, k to end. (22 sts)
Row 30 P.
Cont in st st for 9 rows.
Row 40 Cast off 8 sts, p to end. (14 sts)
Bind off.
Rep for the right front, working arm and neck shaping on the opposite side.

WINTER HAT
Cast on 42 sts in **yarn A** using size 6 (4mm) knitting needles.
Knit 4 rows.
Change to **yarn B**, st st for 4 rows.
Change to **yarn A**, st st for 4 rows.
Change to **yarn B**, st st for 4 rows.
Change to **yarn A**, [k2tog, k1] rep to end. (28 sts)
Row 18 P.
Row 19 [K2tog] rep to end. (14 sts)
Thread yarn through rem sts.

WINTER MITTENS (MAKE 2)
Cast on 14 sts in **yarn A** using size 6 (4mm) knitting needles.
Knit 4 rows.
Change to **yarn B**, st st for 4 rows.
Change to **yarn A**, st st for 4 rows.
Change to **yarn B**, st st for 4 rows.
Change to **yarn A**, [k2tog, k1] rep to last 2 sts, k2tog. (9 sts)
Row 18 P.
Row 19 [k2tog] rep to last st, k1. (5 sts)
Thread yarn through rem sts.

MAKING UP

WINTER COAT
Place the left and right fronts on top of the back of the jacket, right sides out.
Sew the side seams and shoulder seams using thin cream yarn (see Techniques: Making up).
Sew a popper at the neck of the coat and another 1¼in (3cm) below.

WINTER HAT
Sew down the back seam and sew in any loose ends.
Make a small pompom in **yarn B** (see Techniques: Pompoms) and attach it to the top of the hat.

WINTER MITTENS
Fold each mitten in half, right sides out, sew down the seam and sew in any loose ends.
Sew a length of shirring elastic to the cuff of each mitten and thread through the winter coat armholes. You don't want your explorer to loose his mittens!

Explorer Ed plays hide-and-seek

Ed the Explorer was playing hide-and-seek with Joey Kangaroo. He closed his eyes and counted to ten.

"Ready or not, I'm coming to find you," shouted Ed.

Ed started to look. He looked behind some bushes. He looked down a hole in the sand. He even looked in Kath Kangaroo's pouch, but Joey was nowhere to be seen. He didn't notice the little smile on Kath's face. She knew where Joey was hiding!

Ed sat down on a rock to think.

"What's that pinching my bottom?" squeaked Ed.
He turned round sharply and there, behind the rock,
was Joey with a cheeky grin on his face.

Ed always likes a good laugh with friends.

Kath Kangaroo & her baby Joey

Rating

Kath's head, body and legs require a fair amount of shaping and you may find some elements of this project a little fiddly

Kath Kangaroo can jump really high. Joey has to make sure he holds on tight so that he doesn't fall out of his mummy's pouch! They live in Australia, which is sometimes called Down Under, because it's in the southern half of the world.

Kath and Joey are both knitted using the same textured woollen yarn. Fabric details are sewn to their feet, ears and hands. You could have fun choosing a nursery fabric for Joey and a more grown-up fabric for his mother.

Yarn
Medium-weight (Aran) yarn:
1 x 14oz (400g) ball in light brown

Needles
Size 6 (4mm) knitting needles

Gauge
15 sts and 22 rows to 4in (10cm)

Finished sizes
Kath: 12½in (32cm) tall
Joey: 6¼in (16cm) tall

Kath Kangaroo leaps and bounces along.
She stops and spots a quiet billabong.
Inside her pouch Joey's comfy and snug.
He pops his head out and gives Mum a big hug.

Kath Kangaroo pattern

HEAD AND BODY

Starting at the head: cast on 7 sts using size 6 (4mm) knitting needles.
Row 1 [Kfb] 6 times, k1. (13 sts)
Row 2 P.
Row 3 [Kfb, k1, kfb] 4 times, k1. (21 sts)
Row 4 P.
Row 5 [Kfb, k3, kfb] 4 times, k1. (29 sts)
Row 6 P.
Row 7 [Kfb, k5, kfb] 4 times, k1. (37 sts)
Row 8 P.
Row 9 [Kfb, k7, kfb] 4 times, k1. (45 sts)
Row 10 P.
Cont in st st for 10 rows.
Row 21 [K2tog, k7, skpo] 4 times, k1. (37 sts)
Row 22 P.
Row 23 [K2tog, k5, skpo] 4 times, k1. (29 sts)
Row 24 P.

Cont for neck and body:
Cont in st st for 10 rows.
Row 35 [Kfb, k5, kfb] 4 times, k1. (37 sts)
Row 36 P.
Row 37 [Kfb, k7, kfb] 4 times, k1. (45 sts)
Row 38 P.
Row 39 [Kfb, k9, kfb] 4 times, k1. (53 sts)
Row 40 P.
Row 41 [Kfb, k11, kfb] 4 times, k1. (61 sts)
Row 42 P.
Row 43 [Kfb, k13, kfb] 4 times, k1. (69 sts)
Row 44 P.
Cont in st st for 20 rows.
Row 65 [K2tog, k13, skpo] 4 times, k1. (61 sts)
Row 66 P.
Row 67 [K2tog, k11, skpo] 4 times, k1. (53 sts)
Row 68 P.
Row 69 [K2tog, k9, skpo] 4 times, k1. (45 sts)
Row 70 P.
Row 71 [K2tog, k7, skpo] 4 times, k1. (37 sts)
Row 72 P.
Row 73 [K2tog, k5, skpo] 4 times, k1. (29 sts)
Row 74 P.
Row 75 [K2tog, k3, skpo] 4 times, k1. (21 sts)
Row 76 P.
Row 77 [K2tog, k1, skpo] 4 times, k1. (13 sts)
Row 78 P.
Thread yarn through rem sts and pull tight.

NOSE

Cast on 30 sts using size 6 (4mm) knitting needles.
St st for 8 rows.
Row 9 [K1, k2tog] rep to end. (20 sts)
Row 10 P.
Row 11 [K2tog] rep to end. (10 sts)
Thread yarn through rem sts and pull tight.

EARS (MAKE 2)

Cast on 3 sts using size 6 (4mm) knitting needles.
Row 1 Kfb, kfb, k1. (5 sts)
Row 2 P.
Row 3 K.
Row 4 P.
Row 5 K1, kfb, kfb, k2. (7 sts)
Row 6 P.
Row 7 K.
Row 8 P.
Row 9 K2, kfb, kfb, k3. (9 sts)
Row 10 P.
Row 11 K.
Row 12 P.
Thread yarn through rem sts and pull tight.

TAIL

Cast on 36 sts using size 6 (4mm) knitting needles.
Row 1 K.
Row 2 P.
Row 3 K16, skpo, k2tog, k16. (34 sts)
Row 4 P.
Row 5 K15, skpo, k2tog, k15. (32 sts)
Row 6 P.
Row 7 K14, skpo, k2tog, k14. (30 sts)
Row 8 P.
Row 9 K13, skpo, k2tog, k13. (28 sts)
Row 10 P.
Row 11 K12, skpo, k2tog, k12. (26 sts)
Row 12 P.
Cont in st st for 20 rows.
Row 33 [K2tog, k9, skpo] twice. (22 sts)
Row 34 P.
Cont in st st for 4 rows.
Row 39 [K2tog, k7, skpo] twice (18 sts)
Row 40 P.
Cont in st st for 4 rows.
Row 45 [k2tog, k5, skpo] twice. (14 sts)
Row 46 P.
Cont in st st for 4 rows.
Row 51 [K2tog, k3, skpo] 2 times. (10 sts)
Row 52 P.
Cont in st st for 4 rows.
Thread yarn through rem sts and pull tight.

POUCH
Cast on 24 sts using size 6 (4mm) knitting needles.
St st for 24 rows.
Bind off.

ARMS (MAKE 2)
Cast on 6 sts using size 6 (4mm) knitting needles.
Row 1 Kfb, k4, kfb. (8 sts)
Row 2 P.
Row 3 Kfb, k6, kfb. (10 sts)
Row 4 P.
Row 5 Kfb, k8, kfb. (12 sts)
Row 6 P.
Row 7 Kfb, k10, kfb. (14 sts)
Row 8 P.
Cont in st st for 20 rows.
Row 29 [K2tog] rep to end. (7 sts)
Thread yarn through rem sts and pull tight.

LEGS (MAKE 2)
Cast on 19 sts using size 6 (4mm) knitting needles.
Row 1 K8, kfb, kfb, k9. (21 sts)
Row 2 P.
Row 3 K9, kfb, kfb, k10. (23 sts)
Row 4 P.
Row 5 K10, kfb, kfb, k11. (25 sts)
Row 6 P.
Row 7 K11, kfb, kfb, k12. (27 sts)
Row 8 P.
Row 9 K12, kfb, kfb, k13. (29 sts)
Row 10 P.
Cont in st st for 4 rows.
Row 15 K12, skpo, k1, k2tog, k12. (27 sts)
Row 16 P.
Row 17 K11, skpo, k1, k2tog, k11. (25 sts)
Row 18 P.
Row 19 K10, skpo, k1, k2tog, k10. (23 sts)
Row 20 P.
Row 21 K9, skpo, k1, k2tog, k9. (21 sts)
Row 22 P.
Cont in st st for 2 rows.
Row 25 K9, kfb, kfb, k10. (23 sts)
Row 26 P.
Row 27 K14, turn. (9 sts rem)

Cont for top of foot:
Row 28 P5, turn. (9 sts rem)
Row 29 Sl 1, k4, turn.
Row 30 Sl 1, p4, turn.
Rep rows 29 and 30, 5 times.
Hold 5 sts and cut yarn.
Row 41 Start from the inner end of the 9 sts, rejoin yarn, pick up and k7 sts from the right-hand side of the top of the foot, k5 sts (held), pick up and k7 sts from the left-hand side of the top of the foot, k9 sts. (37 sts)

Cont for side of foot:
Row 42 P across 37 sts.
Cont in st st for 4 rows.
Row 47 Skpo twice, k10, skpo twice, k1, k2tog twice, k10, k2tog twice. (29 sts)
Row 48 P.
Bind off.

MAKING UP

HEAD AND BODY

Sew the back seam from each end, leaving an opening of approximately 1⅛in (3cm) in the middle (see Techniques: Making up).
Fill with stuffing.
Sew up the opening.

NOSE

Sew up the seam starting from the tip of the nose.
Loosely fill with stuffing. (Too much stuffing will make the nose look big.)
Stitch the nose to the front of the head using the shaping of the face to position it correctly.

EARS

Cut two patches of fabric for the inner ears (see Templates). Bond fusible interfacing to the wrong side of the fabric.
Neatly sew one pad inside each ear.

ARMS

Fold each arm in half and sew the seam from the paw to under the arm.
Fill with stuffing.
Position the arms correctly at each side of the body and sew, leaving a small opening for stuffing.
Fill to the top of the arm with stuffing and sew up the opening.
Cut two patches of fabric for the paws (see Templates). Bond fusible interfacing to the wrong side of the fabric.
Neatly sew one pad on each paw.

TAIL

Fold the tail in half and sew the seam.
Fill with stuffing.
Position the tail near the base of the kangaroo's back. Use the shaping of the back seam for guidance.
Sew a few gathering stitches along the top of the tail and pull gently to make it bend upwards.

POUCH

Sew the pouch to the lower front of the kangaroo.
Leave an opening at the top to fit Joey in.

LEGS

Fold each leg in half and sew the seam from the heel to the top of the leg.
Fill with stuffing.
Sew up the top of the leg.
Position the legs correctly at the base of the body and sew them on tightly.
Cut two patches of fabric for the feet (see Templates).
Bond fusible interfacing to the wrong side of the fabric.
Neatly sew one pad to the bottom of each foot.

FINISHING TOUCHES

Make the nose by embroidering a number of small knots in pink yarn at the tip of the nose (see Techniques: Embroidering details).
Embroider the mouth and eyes using dark brown or black yarn. Use the shaping of the head to position them correctly and evenly apart.
I added a few stitches of white yarn around the eyes to give them more emphasis.

Baby Joey pattern

HEAD AND BODY

Cast on 7 sts using size 6 (4mm) knitting needles.
Row 1 [Kfb] 6 times, k1. (13 sts)
Row 2 P.
Row 3 [Kfb, k1, kfb] 4 times, k1. (21 sts)
Row 4 P.
Cont in st st for 4 rows.
Row 9 [K2tog, k1, skpo] 4 times, k1. (13 sts)
Row 10 P.
Cont in st st for 4 rows.
Row 15 [Kfb, k1, kfb] 4 times, k1. (21 sts)
Row 16 P.
Row 17 [Kfb, k3, kfb] 4 times, k1. (29 sts)
Row 18 P.
Cont in st st for 8 rows.
Row 27 [K2tog, k3, skpo] 4 times, k1. (21 sts)
Row 28 P.
Row 29 [K2tog, k1, skpo] 4 times, k1. (13 sts)
Row 30 P.
Thread yarn through rem sts and pull tight.

NOSE

Cast on 14 sts using size 6 (4mm) knitting needles.
St st for 3 rows.
Row 4 [P2tog] rep to end. (7 sts)
Thread yarn through rem sts and pull tight.

EARS (MAKE 2)

Cast on 2 sts using size 6 (4mm) knitting needles.
Row 1 Kfb, k1. (3 sts)
Row 2 P.
Row 3 Kfb twice, k1. (5 sts)
Row 4 P.
Row 5 K.
Row 6 P.
Thread yarn through rem sts and pull tight.

TAIL

Cast on 14 sts using size 6 (4mm) knitting needles.
Row 1 K5, skpo, k2tog, k5. (12 sts)
Row 2 P.
Row 3 K.
Row 4 P.
Row 5 K4, skpo, k2tog, k4. (10 sts)
Row 6 P.
Row 7 K.
Row 8 P.
Row 9 [K2tog, k1, skpo] twice. (6 sts)
Row 10 P.
Thread yarn through rem sts and pull tight.

ARMS (MAKE 2)

Cast on 9 sts using size 6 (4mm) knitting needles.
St st for 8 rows.
Row 9 [K2tog] rep to last st, k1. (5 sts)
Thread yarn through rem sts and pull tight.

LEGS (MAKE 2)

Cast on 9 sts using size 6 (4mm) knitting needles.
Row 1 K3, kfb twice, k4. (11 sts)
Row 2 P.
Row 3 K4, kfb twice, k5. (13 sts)
Row 4 P.
Row 5 K.
Row 6 P.
Row 7 K4, skpo, k1, k2tog, k4. (11 sts)
Row 8 P.
Row 9 [K2tog, k1] rep to last 2 sts, k2tog. (7 sts)
Row 10 P.
Cont in st st for 10 rows.
Thread yarn through rem sts and pull tight.

MAKING UP

Make up Joey in the same way as you made Kath, but with fabric patches just on his ears, not his paws. Because he is much smaller, stuff him as you sew him up to make it easier for yourself. When you have sewn and stuffed the leg seams, fold and sew the lower part of each leg so that it bends forward to make the foot. You can then pop little Joey into Kath Kangaroo's pouch, all cosy and warm.

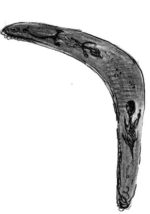

Henry Hippo

Henry's bottom jaw is made separately, which makes his head and body easy to knit

Hippos love keeping cool in mud and water, so they feel most at home in areas of Africa that have some rain, like Zambia. He might make a huge splash, but Henry is a big softy really – just look at the flowers in his ears!

Stuff Henry carefully to give him the correct shape, stitch his lower jaw on accurately to show off his pearly teeth and have fun choosing a pretty floral fabric for his ears and feet.

Yarn
Lightweight (DK) yarn:
2 x 1¾oz (50g) ball in grey (**MC**)
Oddment of pink yarn (**A**)
Oddment of dark brown yarn
Oddment of white yarn

Needles
Size 6 (4mm) knitting needles
Size G/6 (4mm) crochet hook

Gauge
22 sts and 30 rows to 4in (10cm)

Finished size
6¾in (17cm) tall x 11⅜in (29cm) long

Henry the Hippo is feeling very hot.
He waddles to the river, finds a perfect spot.
In he dives and swims around to cool
Then lies down to rest in a little pool.

Henry Hippo pattern

BODY AND HEAD

Starting at hippo's bottom, cast on 8 sts in **yarn MC** using size 6 (4mm) knitting needles.

Row 1 Kfb 8 times. (16 sts)
Row 2 P.
Row 3 Kfb 16 times. (32 sts)
Row 4 P.
Row 5 Kfb 32 times. (64 sts)
Row 6 P.
Cont in st st for 40 rows.
Row 47 [K2tog, k12, skpo] 4 times. (56 sts)
Row 48 P.
Row 49 [K2tog, k10, skpo] 4 times. (48 sts)
Row 50 P.
Row 51 [K2tog, k8, skpo] 4 times. (40 sts)
Row 52 P.
Row 53 [K2tog, k6, skpo] 4 times. (32 sts)
Row 54 P.

Cont for the head:
Row 55 [Kfb, k1] rep to end. (48 sts)
Row 56 P.
Cont in st st for 20 rows.
Row 77 [K2tog, k1] rep to end. (32 sts)
Row 78 P.

Cont for the nose:
St st for 6 rows.
Row 85 K8, [kfb, k1] 8 times, k8. (40 sts)
Row 86 P.
Cont in st st 4 rows.
Row 91 K8, [k2tog, k1] 8 times, k8. (32 sts)
Row 92 P.
Row 93 [K2tog] rep to end. (16 sts)
Row 94 P.
Bind off.

BOTTOM JAW

Cast on 16 sts in **yarn MC** using size 6 (4mm) knitting needles.

St st for 6 rows.

Row 7 Skpo, k12, k2tog. (14 sts)

Row 8 P.

Row 9 Skpo, k10, k2tog. (12 sts)

Row 10 P.

Row 11 Skpo, k8, k2tog. (10 sts)

Row 12 P.

Change to **yarn A**.

Row 13 Kfb, k7, kfb, k1. (12 sts)

Row 14 P.

Row 15 Kfb, k9, kfb, k1. (14 sts)

Row 16 P.

Row 17 Kfb, k11, kfb, k1. (16 sts)

Row 18 P.

Cont in st st for 6 rows.

Bind off.

TEETH (MAKE 2)

Cast on 2 sts in white.

K 1 row.

Bind off.

EARS (MAKE 2)

Cast on 12 sts in **yarn MC**.

St st for 4 rows.

Row 5 [K2tog, k1] rep to end. (8 sts)

Thread the yarn through rem sts and pull tight.

LEGS (MAKE 4)

Cast on 5 sts.

Row 1 [Kfb] rep to end. (10 sts)

Row 2 P.

Row 3 [Kfb] rep to end. (20 sts)

Row 4 K (to form a ridge for toes).

Row 5 K.

Row 6 P.

Cont in st st for 16 rows.

Bind off.

MAKING UP

BODY, HEAD AND BOTTOM JAW

Fold the body in half and sew from the hippo's bottom to the nose shaping. Fill with stuffing. Sew up the bound-off edge.

Fold the bottom jaw in half and sew around the edge so the pink inside jaw lies over the grey outside jaw. Sew the jaw onto the hippo, positioning it accurately below the upper jaw with the pink inside uppermost. Stitch each tooth inside the mouth.

LEGS

Fold each leg in half with knit sides together. Sew from the heel to the top of the leg. Turn right sides out and fill with stuffing.

Secure the legs to the base of the body.

EARS

Fold the ears in half widthways, right sides out, and sew up the back seam. Sew around the edges, pinching in the bottom edge slightly. Attach the ears to the back of the head.

TAIL

Crochet (see Techniques: Crochet chains) 10 chain sts in **yarn MC** using size G/6 (4mm) crochet hook or plait a tail using three strands of yarn for approximately 2in (5cm) long. Attach it to the hippo's rear.

FINISHING TOUCHES

Embroider eyes and a nose in brown and white yarn. Cut four patches of fabric to make the footpads and another two for inner ears (see Templates). Bond fusible interfacing to the wrong side of the fabric. Neatly sew one pad onto the base of each foot and one inside each ear.

Polly the Parrot

Rating

The head involves some colour changing and the legs are a little fiddly

Polly can't help being flamboyant - from her dazzling feathers and amazing voice - because she's Mexican, you know. Life is so full of sunshine, fabulous flowers and lively chatter that she is right at home there.

Most of Polly's plumage is created by simply changing one colour for another. It's just around her face that you'll need to use two colours on the same row - it's not difficult to keep the tension even with some practice.

Yarn
Lightweight (DK) yarn:
1 x 1¾oz (50g) ball in red (**MC**)
1 x 1¾oz (50g) ball in yellow (**A**)
1 x 1¾oz (50g) ball in blue (**B**)
Oddment of cream (**C**)
Oddment of black yarn

Needles
Size 6 (4mm) knitting needles
Size H/8 (5mm) crochet hook

Gauge
22 sts and 30 rows to 4in (10cm)

Finished size
11⅜in (29cm) tall

Polly the parrot is a bright glowing red,
Blue and yellow flashes, and white on her head.
She sits on the treetops and looks all around.
Then flies up in the air with a loud screeching sound.

KNITTING NOTES

When changing from **yarn MC** and **yarn C**, make sure you wrap one yarn around the other to make neat joins. (See Techniques: Intarsia.)

Polly Parrot pattern

HEAD AND BODY
Cast on 9 sts in **yarn MC** using size 6 (4mm) knitting needles.
Row 1 [Kfb, k1] 4 times, k1. (13 sts)
Row 2 P.
Row 3 [Kfb, k1, kfb] 4 times, k1. (21 sts)
Row 4 P.
Row 5 [Kfb, k3, kfb] 4 times, k1. (29 sts)
Row 6 P.
Row 7 [Kfb, k5, kfb] 4 times, k1. (37 sts)
Row 8 P.
Row 9 [Kfb, k7, kfb] 4 times, k1. (45 sts)
Row 10 P.
Cont in patt:
Row 11 K16 in **MC**, k13 in **C**, k16 in **MC**.
Row 12 P15 in **MC**, p15 in **C**, p15 in **MC**.
Row 13 K14 in **MC**, k17 in **C**, k14 in **MC**.
Row 14 P13 in **MC**, p19 in **C**, p13 in **MC**.
Row 15 K12 in **MC**, k21 in **C**, k12 in **MC**.
Row 16 P11 in **MC**, p23 in **C**, p11 in **MC**.
Row 17 K11 in **MC**, k23 in **C**, k11 in **MC**.
Row 18 P12 in **MC**, p21 in **C**, p12 in **MC**.
Row 19 K13 in **MC**, k19 in **C**, k13 in **MC**.
Row 20 P14 in **MC**, p17 in **C**, p14 in **MC**.
Row 21 K15 in **MC**, k15 in **C**, k15 in **MC**.
Row 22 P16 in **MC**, p13 in **C**, p16 in **MC**.
Cont in **yarn MC**:
Row 23 K.
Row 24 P.

Row 25 [K2tog, k7, skpo] 4 times, k1. (37 sts)
Row 26 P.
Row 27 [K2tog, k5, skpo] 4 times, k1. (29 sts)
Row 28 P.
Row 29 [Kfb, k1] rep to last st, kfb. (44 sts)
Row 30 P.

Cont for body:
Row 31 K.
Row 32 P.
Row 33 K.
Row 34 P.
Row 35 Kfb, k19, kfb twice, k20, kfb, k1. (48 sts)
Row 36 P.
Row 37 K.
Row 38 P.
Row 39 Kfb, k21, kfb twice, k22, kfb, k1. (52 sts)
Row 40 P.
Cont in st st for 12 rows.
Row 53 [K2tog, k9, skpo] 4 times. (44 sts)
Row 54 P.
Row 55 [K2tog, k7, skpo] 4 times. (36 sts)
Row 56 P.
Row 57 [K2tog, k5, skpo] 4 times. (28 sts)
Row 58 P.
Row 59 [K2tog, k3, skpo] 4 times. (20 sts)
Row 60 P.
Row 61 [K2tog, k1, skpo] 4 times. (12 sts)
Row 62 P.
Thread yarn through rem sts and pull tight.

BEAK (MAKE 2)
Cast on 12 sts in black yarn using size 6 (4mm)
knitting needles.
Row 1 K4, skpo, k2tog, k4. (10 sts)
Row 2 P.
Change to **yarn A**.
Row 3 K3, skpo, k2tog, k3. (8 sts)
Row 4 P.
Row 5 K2, skpo, k2tog, k2. (6 sts)
Row 6 P.
Row 7 K1, skpo, k2tog, k1. (4 sts)
Row 8 P.
Thread yarn through rem sts and pull tight.

WING (MAKE 4)
Cast on 3 sts in **yarn MC** using size 6 (4mm)
knitting needles.
Row 1 Kfb, kfb, k1. (5 sts)
Row 2 P.
Row 3 K1, kfb twice, k2. (7 sts)
Row 4 P.
Row 5 K2, kfb twice, k3. (9 sts)
Row 6 P.
Row 7 K3, kfb twice, k4. (11 sts)
Row 8 P.
Row 9 K4, kfb twice, k5. (13 sts)
Row 10 P.
Change to **yarn A**.
Row 11 K5, kfb twice, k6. (15 sts)
Row 12 P.
Row 13 K6, kfb twice, k7. (17 sts)
Row 14 P.
Row 15 K.
Row 16 P.
Row 17 K.
Row 18 P.
Row 19 K.
Row 20 P.
Change to **yarn B**.
Row 21 K.
Row 22 P.
Row 23 Skpo, k13, k2tog. (15 sts)
Row 24 P.
Row 25 Skpo, k11, k2tog. (13 sts)
Row 26 P.
Cont decr on alternate rows until 3 sts rem.
Thread yarn through rem sts and pull tight.

TAIL (MAKE 2)
Cast on 16 sts in **yarn MC** using size 6 (4mm) knitting needles.
Row 1 K.
Row 2 P.
Row 3 K.
Row 4 P.
Change to **yarn A**.
Row 5 K6, skpo, k2tog, k6. (14 sts)
Row 6 P.
Row 7 K.
Row 8 P.
Row 9 K5, skpo, k2tog, k5. (12 sts)
Row 10 P.
Row 11 K.
Row 12 P.
Change to **yarn B**.
Row 13 K4, skpo, k2tog, k4. (10 sts)
Row 14 P.
Row 15 K.
Row 16 P.
Row 17 K3, skpo, k2tog, k3. (8 sts)
Row 18 P
Cont in st st for 6 rows.
Change to **yarn MC**.
Row 25 K.
Row 26 P.
Cont in st st for 4 rows.
Bind off.

FEET (MAKE 2)
Cast on 3 sts in black yarn using size 6 (4mm) knitting needles. Leave a long end of yarn to crochet the legs later.
Row 1 Kfb twice, k1. (5 sts)
Row 2 P.
Row 3 K1, kfb twice, k2. (7 sts)
Row 4 P.
Row 5 K2, kfb twice, k3. (9 sts)
Row 6 P.
Row 7 K3, kfb twice, k4. (11 sts)
Row 8 P.
Row 9 K4, kfb twice, k5. (13 sts)
Row 10 P.
Row 11 K4, skpo, k1, k2tog, k4. (11 sts)
Row 12 P.
Row 13 K3, skpo, k1, k2tog, k3. (9 sts)
Row 14 P.
Row 15 K2, skpo, k1, k2tog, k2. (7 sts)
Row 16 P.
Row 17 K1, skpo, k1, k2tog, k1. (5 sts)
Thread yarn through rem sts and pull tight.
Cut yarn, leaving approx 12in (30cm) end of yarn to crochet the legs later.

MAKING UP

HEAD AND BODY
Fold the head and body in half and sew from each end, leaving an opening in the middle. Fill with stuffing and sew up the opening.

BEAK
Sew the two pieces together to make the top and bottom of the beak. Fill with stuffing.
Position the beak correctly across the cream part of the parrot's face. Sew it securely in place.

WINGS
Sew two pieces together for each wing, leaving an opening on one side. Fill very loosely with stuffing and sew up the openings.
Position the wings on each side of the body just below the neck with the blue points facing downwards.

TAIL
Sew the two pieces together to make the top and bottom of the tail, leaving the wider end open. Fill loosely with stuffing. Position the open end of the tail on the rear of the parrot and sew in place.

FEET AND LEGS
Fold each foot in half and sew around the edges. Use the two loose ends and size H/8 (5mm) crochet hook to make a crochet chain of 5 sts (see Techniques: Crochet chains).
Securely attach the two legs to the base of the body.

FINISHING TOUCHES
Embroider eyes using black yarn.

Polly Parrot sings in the jungle

Polly Parrot has a beautiful singing voice. Every afternoon she flies to the tallest tree to give her best performance to entertain the other birds and animals.

She sings and sings at the top of her voice. Animals travel from far and wide to watch and hear her sing. It really is a show-stopping performance.

At 4 o'clock each day Monkey Mike, along with his monkey mates, swings from branch to branch until he finds the perfect position to hear her perform. As Monkey Mike and his friends stop their chattering, silence descends. Mike lies back on a branch and makes himself comfortable. Then Polly begins and the air is filled with sweet music.

Monkey Mike

Rating

Practise two-colour intarsia so the face and tummy will give you no problems

Monkey Mike is a natural exhibitionist, so he puts on an astoundingly acrobatic show in his native Brazil. His antics are sure to be loved by all and he's very affectionate when he's not monkeying around.

Once you have mastered the colour changes for Mike's head and body, the rest of him will come together easily. Then you can have fun choosing some jolly fabric for Mike's feet and ears, to bring out his cheeky character.

Yarn
Medium-weight (Aran) yarn:
1 x 1¾oz (50g) ball in dark fawn (**MC**)
1 x 1¾oz (50g) ball in light fawn (**A**)
Oddment of dark brown yarn

Needles
Size 5 (3.75mm) knitting needles

Gauge
17 sts and 21 rows to 4in (10cm)

Finished size
13¾in (35cm) tall

Monkey Mike swings through the trees.
He stretches his arms and grabs the green leaves.
He looks for bananas and spots a huge bunch.
He swings up to reach them and soon starts to munch.

When changing from
yarn MC and **yarn A**,
make sure you wrap one
yarn around the other
to make neat joins. (See
Techniques, intarsia.)

Monkey Mike pattern

HEAD, BODY, LEGS AND FEET

Starting at head, cast on 9 sts in **yarn MC** using size
5 (3.75mm) knitting needles.
Row 1 [Kfb, k1] 4 times, k1. (13 sts)
Row 2 P.
Row 3 [Kfb, k1, kfb] 4 times, k1. (21 sts)
Row 4 P.
Row 5 [Kfb, k3, kfb] 4 times, k1. (29 sts)
Row 6 P.
Cont in patt:
Row 7 [Kfb, k5, kfb twice, k4] in **MC**; [k1, kfb twice,
k2] in **A**; [k3, kfb twice, k5, kfb, k1] in **MC**. (37 sts)
Row 8 P14 in **MC**; p9 in **A**; p14 in **MC**.
Row 9 [Kfb, k7, kfb twice, k3] in **MC**; [k4, kfb twice,
k5] in **A**; [k2, kfb twice, k7, kfb, k1] in **MC**. (45 sts)
Row 10 P16 in **MC**; p13 in **A**; p16 in **MC**.
Row 11 K14 in **MC**; k17 in **A**; k14 in **MC**.

Row 12 P12 in **MC**; p21 in **A**; p12 in **MC**.
Row 13 K11 in **MC**; k23 in **A**; k11 in **MC**.
Row 14 P11 in **MC**; p23 in **A**; p11 in **MC**.
Row 15 K11 in **MC**; k23 in **A**; k11 in **MC**.
Row 16 P11 in **MC**; p23 in **A**; p11 in **MC**.
Row 17 [K2tog, k7, skpo] in **MC**; [k2tog, k7, skpo, k1,
k2tog, k7, skpo] in **A**; [k2tog, k7, skpo] in **MC**. (37 sts)
Row 18 P10 in **MC**; p17 in **A**; p10 in **MC**.
Row 19 [K2tog, k5, skpo, k2tog] in **MC**; [k5, skpo, k1,
k2tog, k5] in **A**; [skpo, k2tog, k5, skpo] in **MC**. (29 sts)

Cont for body in **yarn MC**:
Row 20 P.
Row 21 K.
Row 22 P.
Row 23 [Kfb, k5, kfb] 4 times, k1. (37 sts)
Row 24 P.

Cont in patt:

Row 25 [Kfb, k7, kfb twice, k2] in **MC**; [k5, kfb twice, k5] in **A**; [k2, kfb twice, k7, kfb, k1] in **MC**. (45 sts)

Row 26 P15 in **MC**; p16 in **A**; p14 in **MC**.

Row 27 [Kfb, k9, kfb twice, k1] in **MC**; [k8, kfb twice, k8] in **A**; [k1, kfb twice, k9, kfb, k1] in **MC**. (53 sts)

Row 28 P16 in **MC**; p22 in **A**; p15 in **MC**.

Row 29 K15 in **MC**; k22 in **A**; k16 in **MC**.

Row 30 P16 in **MC**; p22 in **A**; p15 in **MC**.

Rep rows 29 and 30, 5 times.

Cont in **yarn MC**:

Row 41 [K2tog, k9, skpo] 4 times, k1. (45 sts)

Row 42 P.

Row 43 [K2tog, k7, skpo] 4 times, k1. (37 sts)

Row 44 P.

Row 45 [K2tog, k5, skpo] 4 times, k1. (29 sts)

Row 46 P.

Row 47 [K2tog, k4] 4 times, k2tog, k3. (24 sts)

Row 48 P12, turn. Leave rem sts on stitch holder.

Cont for leg:
St st on 12 sts for 30 rows.

Cont for foot:

Row 79 K5, kfb, kfb, k5. (14 sts)

Row 80 P.

Row 81 K6, kfb twice, k6. (16 sts)

Row 82 P.

Row 83 K7, kfb twice, k7. (18 sts)

Row 84 P.

Row 85 K8, kfb twice, k8. (20 sts)

Row 86 P.

Row 87 [K2tog] rep to end. (10 sts)

Thread yarn through rem sts and pull tight.

Rep leg and foot patt on rem 12 sts from row 48.

ARMS AND HANDS (MAKE 2)

Cast on 12 sts in **yarn MC** using size 5 (3.75mm) knitting needles.

St st for 30 rows.

Cont for hands:

Row 31 K2, kfb, k5, kfb, k3. (14 sts)

Row 32 P.

St st for 4 rows.

Row 37 [K2tog] rep to end. (7 sts)

Thread yarn through rem sts and pull tight.

EARS (MAKE 2)

Cast on 16 sts in **yarn MC** using size 5 (3.75mm) knitting needles.

St st for 4 rows.

Row 5 [K2tog] rep to end. (8 sts)

Thread yarn through rem sts and pull tight.

TAIL

Cast on 10 sts in **yarn MC** using size 5 (3.75mm) knitting needles.

St st for 30 rows.

Row 31 [K1, k2tog] rep to last st, k1. (7 sts)

Row 32 P.

Row 33 K.

Row 34 P.

Thread yarn through rem sts and pull tight.

MAKING UP

HEAD AND BODY
Sew up from the top of the head to the base of the body, leaving an opening for stuffing. Fill with stuffing and sew up the opening.

LEGS AND FEET
Sew up from each end, leaving an opening in the middle for stuffing. Fill with stuffing and sew up the opening.

ARMS AND HANDS
Sew up from each end, leaving an opening in the middle for stuffing. Fill with stuffing and sew up the opening.
Sew the arms onto the body using the shaping to position them correctly.

EARS
Fold each ear in half with the seam at the centre back and sew around the edges, slightly pinching in the side that attaches to the head. Sew the ears onto the head using the shaping to position them correctly.

TAIL
Fold the tail in half and sew the two long edges together, leaving an opening for stuffing. Fill with stuffing and sew up the opening.
Sew the tail onto the base of the body.

FINISHING TOUCHES
Embroider the mouth, nose and eyes in place using dark brown yarn.
Cut four patches of fabric to make the footpads and another two for inner ears (see Templates). Bond fusible interfacing to the wrong side of the fabric. Neatly sew one pad onto the base of each foot and one inside each ear.

Timothy Tiger

With simple shapes, the interest is created by working with multi-coloured yarn and stripes

Timothy lives in India, though he has cousins in other parts of Asia. He has a fearsome reputation and it would be best to keep him sweet with lots of treats and cuddles.

You could easily use this pattern to make other members of the cat family from domestic friends to pumas, cheetahs or even an elusive snow leopard. Just choose your favourite and the appropriate colours of yarn.

Yarn
Lightweight (DK) yarn:
1 x 1¾oz (50g) ball in multi-
coloured ginger (**MC**)
1 x 1¾oz (50g) ball in black (**A**)
1 x 1¾oz (50g) ball in white (**B**)

Needles
Size 6 (4mm) knitting needles

Gauge
22 sts and 30 rows to 4in (10cm)

Finished size
5½in (14cm) tall x 8⅝in (22cm) long (including tail)

Timothy Tiger licks his lips.
He stands up tall and wiggles his hips.
Then Timothy Tiger sharpens each claw.
He opens his mouth and gives a loud roar.

Timothy Tiger pattern

HEAD AND BODY

Starting at nose, cast on 6 sts in **yarn MC** using size 6 (4mm) knitting needles.

Row 1 Kfb 5 times, k1. (11 sts)
Row 2 P.
Row 3 Kfb 10 times, k1. (21 sts)
Row 4 P.
Row 5 K2, [kfb, k4] 3 times, kfb, k3. (25 sts)
Row 6 P.
Row 7 K2, kfb, k6, kfb, k4, kfb, k6, kfb, k3. (29 sts)
Row 8 P.
Row 9 K2, kfb, k8, kfb, k4, kfb, k8, kfb, k3. (33 sts)
Row 10 P.
Row 11 K2, kfb, k10, kfb, k4, kfb, k10, kfb, k3. (37 sts)
Row 12 P.
Row 13 K2, kfb, k12, kfb, k4, kfb, k12, kfb, k3. (41 sts)
Row 14 P.
Row 15 K2, kfb, k14, kfb, k4, kfb, k14, kfb, k3. (45 sts)
Row 16 P.

Row 17 K.
Row 18 P.
Row 19 K2, skpo, k14, skpo, k5, k2tog, k14, k2tog, k2. (41 sts)
Row 20 P.
Row 21 K2, skpo, k12, skpo, k5, k2tog, k12, k2tog, k2. (37 sts)
Row 22 P.
Change to **yarn A**.
Row 23 K2, skpo, k10, skpo, k5, k2tog, k10, k2tog, k2. (33 sts)
Row 24 P.
Change to **yarn MC**.
Row 25 K2, skpo, k8, skpo, k5, k2tog, k8, k2tog, k2. (29 sts)
Row 26 P.
Row 27 K.
Row 28 P.

Cont for body:
Change to **yarn A**.
Row 29 K1, [kfb, k1] rep to end. (43 sts)
Row 30 P.
Cont in st st for 24 rows in stripe patt, alternating 4 rows of **yarn MC**, 2 rows of **yarn A**, to end of body.
Cont in **yarn MC**.
Row 55 K1, [k2tog, k1] rep to end. (29 sts)
Row 56 P.
Row 57 K1, [k2tog] rep to end. (15 sts)
Row 58 P.
Thread yarn through rem 15 sts and pull tight to form tiger's bottom.

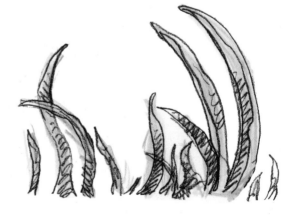

OUTER EAR (MAKE 2)

Cast on 12 sts in **yarn A** using size 6 (4mm) knitting needles.

Row 1 K.

Change to **yarn MC**.

Row 2 P.

Row 3 K.

Change to **yarn A**.

Row 4 P.

Row 5 K1, [k2tog, k1, k2tog] twice, k1. (8 sts)

Change to **yarn MC**.

Row 6 P.

Row 7 K2tog, k4, k2tog. (6 sts)

Row 8. P.

Row 9. K.

Bind off.

INNER EAR (MAKE 2)

Cast on 10 sts in **yarn B** using size 6 (4mm) knitting needles.

Row 1 K.

Row 2 P.

Row 3 K.

Row 4 P.

Row 5 K1 [k2 tog, k1] rep to end. (7 sts)

Row 6 P.

Row 7 K.

Bind off.

NOSE AND MUZZLE

Cast on 6 sts in **yarn MC** using size 6 (4mm) knitting needles.

Row 1 K.
Row 2 P.
Row 3 K1, kfb 4 times, k1. (10 sts)
Row 4 P.
Row 5 K1, kfb 8 times, k1. (18 sts)
Row 6 P.
Row 7 K.
Row 8 P.
Change to **yarn B**.
Row 9 K.
Row 10 P.
Row 11 K.
Row 12 P.
Row 13 K1, k2tog 8 times, k1. (10 sts)
Row 14 P.
Row 15 K1, k2tog 4 times, k1. (6 sts)
Row 16 P.
Thread yarn through rem sts and pull tight.

LEGS (MAKE 4)

Cast on 17 sts in **yarn MC** using size 6 (4mm) knitting needles.

St st for 12 rows in stripe patt: 4 rows **yarn MC**, 2 rows **yarn A**.
Cont in patt:
Row 13 K7, kfb, kfb, k8. (19 sts)
Row 14 P.
Row 15 K8, kfb, kfb, k9. (21 sts)
Row 16 P.
Row 17 K9, kfb, kfb, k10. (23 sts)
Row 18 P.
Row 19 K2tog, k19, k2tog. (21 sts)
Row 20 P.
Row 21 [K1, k2tog] rep to end. (14 sts)
Row 22 P.
Row 23 [K2tog] rep to end. (7 sts)
Thread yarn through rem sts and pull tight.

TAIL

Cast on 10 sts in **yarn MC** using size 6 (4mm) knitting needles.

St st for 24 rows in stripe patt: 4 rows **yarn MC**, 2 rows **yarn A**.
Change to **yarn B**.
Row 25 K.
Row 26 P.
Row 27 K.
Row 28 P.
Row 29 [K2tog] rep to end. (5 sts)
Thread yarn through rem sts and pull tight.

MAKING UP

HEAD AND BODY
Sew from each end, leaving an opening in the middle. Fill with stuffing and sew up the opening.

NOSE AND MUZZLE
Position the nose and muzzle using the shaping on the face, so that the ginger section is on top and the white section is underneath. Sew all around the edges, leaving a small opening. Loosely fill with stuffing and sew up the opening.

EARS
Neatly stitch one white inner ear to each stripy outer ear, right sides out.
Sew the ears on each side of the tiger's head using the shaping at the top of the head to position them correctly.

LEGS
Sew from the heel to the top of each leg. Fill with stuffing.
Position the legs under the tiger's body and sew them on securely.

TAIL
Neatly stitch the long sides together, stuffing the tail as you go.
Sew the stripy end of the tail to the rear of the tiger.

FINISHING TOUCHES
Embroider the tiger's eyes in black yarn and then outline them in white yarn to add definition.
Embroider his nose, whisker dots and mouth using black yarn.
Cut four patches of fabric to make the footpads (see Templates). Bond fusible interfacing to the wrong side of the fabric. Neatly sew each pad onto the base of each foot.

Explorer Ed gets lost in a forest

Ed the Explorer was marching through a forest in China.

There were strange looking trees everywhere; trees to

the front of him, trees to the right, trees to the left

and trees behind him. Ed quickly realized that these

were not trees at all but very large bamboo canes.

"Oh no, I'm lost," said Ed.

He stopped to check his map when suddenly he heard

a munching sound coming from behind one of the

bamboo canes. He slowly crept towards the sound and peered

round the cane feeling a bit afraid of what he might find.

Sitting on the floor munching and crunching away on

a bamboo shoot was Penny the Panda.

Ed always smiles when he finds a new friend.

Penny the Panda

Rating

All of the pieces for this lovely toy are made separately and sewn together at the end

It is very rare to see a panda bear like Penny. She lives in China. She is shy and likes to hide away from people so they can't find her. But you can always tell when she is near, because of the munching sounds as she chews her bamboo.

You can change the appearance of this bear completely, simply by using different colour combinations of yarn. You could knit the body in brown and the tummy in white. Try to use a soft yarn to make your bear really cuddly.

Yarn
Lightweight (DK) yarn:
1 x 3½oz (100g) ball in black (**A**)
1 x 3½oz (100g) ball in white (**B**)

Needles
Size 6 (4mm) knitting needles

Gauge
22 sts and 30 rows to 4in (10cm)

Finished sizes
12in (30cm) tall

Penny the panda sits under the trees
And looks at the sky through the bright-coloured leaves.
She greedily munches some green bamboo shoots
And nibbles them all right down to the roots.

Penny the Panda pattern

BODY

Cast on 9 sts in **yarn A**, using size 6 (4mm) knitting needles.

Row 1 [Kfb, k1] 4 times, k1. (13 sts)
Row 2 P.
Row 3 [Kfb, k1, kfb] 4 times, k1. (21 sts)
Row 4 P.
Row 5 [Kfb, k3, kfb] 4 times, k1. (29 sts)
Row 6 P.
Row 7 [Kfb, k5, kfb] 4 times, k1. (37 sts)
Row 8 P.
Row 9 [Kfb, k7, kfb] 4 times, k1. (45 sts)
Row 10 P.
Row 11 [Kfb, k9, kfb] 4 times, k1. (53 sts)
Row 12 P.
Row 13 [Kfb, k11, kfb] 4 times, k1. (61 sts)
Row 14 P.
Change to **yarn B.**
Cont in st st for 20 rows.
Row 35 [K2tog] rep to last st, k1. (31 sts)
Row 36 P.
Row 37 [K2tog] rep to last st, k1. (16 sts)
Row 38 P.
Row 39 [K2tog] rep to end. (8 sts)
Thread yarn through rem sts and pull tight.

HEAD

Cast on 9 sts in **yarn B**, using size 6 (4mm) knitting needles.

Row 1 [Kfb, k1] 4 times, k1. (13 sts)
Row 2 P.
Row 3 [Kfb, k1, kfb] 4 times, k1. (21 sts)
Row 4 P.
Row 5 [Kfb, k3, kfb] 4 times, k1. (29 sts)
Row 6 P.
Row 7 [Kfb, k5, kfb] 4 times, k1. (37 sts)
Row 8 P.
Row 9 [Kfb, k7, kfb] 4 times, k1. (45 sts)
Row 10 P.
Row 11 [Kfb, k9, kfb] 4 times, k1. (53 sts)
Row 12 P.
Row 13 K.
Row 14 P.

EYES

Row 15 K17 in **B**, k6 in **A**, k7 in **B**, k6 in **A**, k17 in **B**.
Row 16 P16 in **B**, p8 in **A**, p5 in **B**, p8 in **A**, p17 in **B**.
Row 17 K15 in **B**, k9 in **A**, k5 in **B**, k9 in **A**, k17 in **B**.
Row 18 P15 in **B**, p9 in **A**, p5 in **B**, p9 in **A**, p17 in **B**.
Row 19 K16 in **B**, k8 in **A**, k5 in **B**, k8 in **A**, k17 in **B**.
Row 20 P17 in **B**, p6 in **A**, p7 in **B**, p6 in **A**, p17 in **B**.
Cont in st st for 8 rows in **yarn B**.
Row 29 [K2tog] rep to last st, k1. (27 sts)
Row 30 P.
Row 31 [K2tog] rep to last st, k1. (14 sts)
Row 32 P.
Row 33 [K2tog] rep to end. (7 sts)
Thread yarn through rem sts and pull tight.

NOSE

Cast on 30 sts in **yarn B** using size 6 (4mm)
knitting needles.
St st for 6 rows.
Row 7 [K1, k2tog] rep to end of row. (20 sts)
Row 8 P.
Row 9 [K2tog] rep to end of row. (10 sts)
Thread yarn through rem sts and pull together.

EARS (MAKE 2)

Cast on 26 sts in **yarn A** using size 6 (4mm)
knitting needles.
St st for 5 rows.
Row 6 [P2tog, p1] rep to last 2 sts, p2tog. (17 sts)
Row 7 K.
Row 8 [P2tog] rep to last st, p1. (9 sts)
Thread yarn through rem sts and pull tight.

ARMS (MAKE 2)

Cast on 10 sts in **yarn A** using size 6 (4mm)
knitting needles.
Row 1 Kfb, k8, kfb. (12 sts)
Row 2 P.
Row 3 Kfb, k10, kfb. (14 sts)
Row 4 P.
Cont in this way until 22 sts on needle.
Row 13 K.
Row 14 P.
Cont in st st for 18 rows.
Row 33 [K1, k2tog] rep to last st, k1. (15 sts)
Row 34 P.
Row 35 [K2tog] rep to last st, k1. (8 sts)
Thread yarn through rem sts and pull tight.

LEGS (MAKE 2)

Cast on 25 sts in **yarn A** using size 6 (4mm)
knitting needles.
St st for 20 rows.
Row 21 K11, kfb twice, k12. (27 sts)
Row 22 P.
Row 23 K12, kfb twice, k13. (29 sts)
Row 24 P.
Row 25 K13, kfb twice, k14. (31 sts)
Row 26 P.
Row 27 K14, kfb twice, k15. (33 sts)
Row 28 P.
Row 29 K15, kfb twice, k16. (35 sts)
Row 30 P.
Row 31 K2tog, k31, k2tog. (33 sts)
Row 32 P.
Row 33 [K2tog, k1] rep to end. (22 sts)
Row 34 P.
Row 35 [K2tog] rep to end. (11 sts)
Thread yarn through rem sts and pull together.

MAKING UP

BODY

Sew the back body seam from each end, leaving an opening of approximately 1⅛in (3cm) in the middle (see Techniques: Making up).
Fill with stuffing.
Sew up the opening.

HEAD

Sew the rear head seam from each end, leaving an opening of approximately 1¼in (3cm) in the middle.
Fill with stuffing.
Sew up the opening.

NOSE

Sew up the seam starting from the tip of nose.
Loosely fill with stuffing. (Too much stuffing will make the nose look big.)
Stitch the nose to the front of the head using the black eye patches to position it correctly.

EARS

Fold each ear in half, right sides out, and sew up the back seam. This gives you a chunky, double-sided ear. Sew along the bottom straight edge and pull gently to give the ear its curved shape.
Cut out two iron-on interfacing-lined fabric ear patches (see Templates).

Sew each piece of fabric to the inside of one knitted ear (see Techniques: Appliqués).
Stitch one ear to each side of the panda's head using the shaping at the top of the head to position them correctly and evenly apart.

ARMS
Fold each arm in half, right sides out, and sew the seam from the hand to under the arm.
Fill with stuffing.
Position the arms correctly at each side of the body and sew, leaving a small opening for stuffing.
Fill to top of the arm with stuffing and sew up the opening.
Cut two patches of fabric for the paws (see Templates).
Bond fusible interfacing to the wrong side of the fabric.
Neatly sew one pad on each paw.

LEGS
Fold each leg in half and sew the seam from the heel to the top of the leg.
Fill with stuffing.
Position the legs correctly at the base of the body and sew them on tightly.
Cut two patches of fabric for the feet (see Templates).
Bond fusible interfacing to the wrong side of the fabric.
Neatly sew one pad to the bottom of each foot.

FINISHING TOUCHES
Embroider the panda's nose and mouth using black yarn (see Techniques: Embroidering details).
Embroider eyes in the centre of the black eye patches.

Mummy & Baby Meerkat

Rating ⚬⚬⚬⚬⚬ ⚬⚬⚬⚬⚬ ⚬⚬⚬⚬⚬

*Practise getting the shaping right with Mum before you
tackle Baby who, being smaller, is a bit more fiddly*

Baby Meerkat is such a bundle of fun - always tumbling around on the dry
grasslands and deserts that are his home in Namibia in West Africa. His
mother is always on the look out to keep her baby safe from danger.

Stuff the limbs to give plenty of flexibility so these inquisitive animals
can have lots of fun. Then have a go at giving them different
expressions - a kindly smile for Mum and a cheeky grin for Baby.

Yarn
Lightweight (DK) yarn:
1 x 1¾oz (50g) ball in oatmeal (**MC**)
Oddment of black yarn (**A**)
Oddment of white yarn

Needles
Size 6 (4mm) knitting needles

Gauge
22 sts and 30 rows to 4in (10cm)

Finished sizes
Mummy: 15¼in (39cm) tall
Baby: 10½in (27cm) tall

Mummy Meerkat looks all around.
She's searching for Baby who cannot be found.
Then up he pops from a hole in the sand.
He hops and jumps and waves his hand.

Mummy Meerkat pattern

HEAD, BODY AND LEGS

Starting at nose, cast on 7 sts in yarn **MC** using size 6 (4mm) knitting needles.

Row 1 Kfb 6 times, k1. (13 sts)
Row 2 P.
Row 3 [Kfb, k1, kfb] 4 times, k1. (21 sts)
Row 4 P.
Row 5 [Kfb, k3, kfb] 4 times, k1. (29 sts)
Row 6 P.
Row 7 [Kfb, k5, kfb] 4 times, k1. (37 sts)
Row 8 P.
Row 9 [Kfb, k7, kfb] 4 times, k1. (45 sts)
Row 10 P.
Row 11 K20, kfb 4 times, k21. (49 sts)
Row 12 P.
Row 13 K22, kfb 4 times, k23. (53 sts)
Row 14 P.
Row 15 K24, kfb 4 times, k25. (57 sts)
Row 16 P.
Row 17 K26, kfb 4 times, k27. (61 sts)
Row 18 P.
Row 19 K26, skpo twice, k1, k2tog twice, k26. (57 sts)
Row 20 P.
Row 21 K24, skpo twice, k1, k2tog twice, k24. (53 sts)
Row 22 P.
Row 23 K22, skpo twice, k1, k2tog twice, k22. (49 sts)
Row 24 P.
Row 25 K20, skpo twice, k1, k2tog twice, k20. (45 sts)
Row 26 P.
Row 27 [K2tog, k7, skpo] 4 times, k1. (37 sts)
Row 28 P.
Row 29 [K2tog, k5, skpo] 4 times, k1. (29 sts)
Row 30 P.

Cont for neck and body:
Row 31 [K2tog, k3, skpo] 4 times, k1. (21 sts)
Row 32 P.
Cont in st st for 6 rows.
Row 39 [Kfb, k3, kfb] 4 times, k1. (29 sts)
Row 40 P.
Row 41 [Kfb, k5, kfb] 4 times, k1. (37 sts)
Row 42 P.
Row 43 [Kfb, k7, kfb] 4 times, k1. (45 sts)
Row 44 P.
Row 45 [Kfb, k9, kfb] 4 times, k1. (53 sts)
Row 46 P.

Row 47 [Kfb, k11, kfb] 4 times, k1. (61 sts)
Row 48 P.
Cont in st st for 20 rows.
Row 69 [Kfb, k13, kfb] 4 times, k1. (69 sts)
Row 70 P.
Cont in st st for 6 rows.
Row 77 [Kfb, k15, kfb] 4 times, k1. (77 sts)
Row 78 P.
Cont in st st for 6 rows.
Row 85 [K2tog, k15, skpo] 4 times, k1. (69 sts)
Row 86 P.
Row 87 [K2tog, k13, skpo] 4 times, k1. (61 sts)

KNITTING NOTES

Don't worry if the gauge is not exact. It doesn't matter if your meerkats are a bit bigger or smaller than mine.

Row 88 P.
Row 89 [K2tog, k11, skpo] 4 times, k1. (53 sts)
Row 90 P.
Row 91 [K2tog, k9, skpo] 4 times, k1. (45 sts)
Row 92 P.
Row 93 [K2tog, k7, skpo] 4 times, k1. (37 sts)
Row 94 P.

Cont for right leg:
Row 95 K18, turn.
Row 96 P18.
Cont in st st for 30 rows.
Row 127 [K2tog] rep to end. (9 sts)
Thread yarn through rem sts and pull tight.
Cont for left leg, picking up 19 rem sts:
Row 95 K2tog, k17. (18 sts)
Row 96 P18.
Rep as for right leg.

EARS (MAKE 2)
Cast on 12 sts in yarn **A** using size 6 (4mm) knitting needles.
St st for 3 rows.
Row 4 [P2tog] rep to end. (6 sts)
Thread yarn through rem sts and pull tight.

TAIL
Cast on 16 sts in yarn **MC** using size 6 (4mm) knitting needles.
St st for 30 rows.
Row 31 [K1, k2tog] rep to last st, k1. (11 sts)
Row 32 P.
Row 33 K.
Row 34 P.
Thread yarn through rem sts and pull tight.

ARMS (MAKE 2)
Cast on 14 sts in yarn **MC** using size 6 (4mm) knitting needles.
St st for 40 rows.
Row 41 [K2tog] rep to end. (7 sts)
Row 42 P.
Thread yarn through rem sts and pull tight.

EYES (MAKE 2)
Cast on 8 sts in yarn **A** using size 6 (4mm) knitting needles.
Row 1 P.
Row 2 K1, kfb, k4, kfb, k1. (10 sts)
Row 3 P.
Row 4 K.
Row 5 P.
Row 6 K1, k2tog, k4, k2tog, k1. (8 sts)
Row 7 P.
Bind off.

MAKING UP

HEAD, BODY AND LEGS

Starting at the toes, sew up the leg seams, stuffing as you go.

Sew from each end of the back seam, leaving approximately 1⅛in (3cm) opening in the middle. Fill with stuffing and then sew up the opening.

To form the feet, fold over 2in (5cm) from the toes and stitch the top of each foot to the ankle.

EARS

Fold in half and sew together the cast-on edge at the bottom of the ear. Pull the stitching slightly to curve the base of the ear.

Stitch one ear to each side of the head using the shaping at the top of the head to position them evenly.

ARMS

Fold in half and sew the seam from the hand to the underarm. Fill with stuffing.

Position one arm on each side of the body using the neck shaping as a guide.

To form the forearms, fold over 2in (5cm) from the fingers and stitch to form each elbow.

TAIL

Fold in half and sew the seam. Fill with stuffing. Position the tail near the base of the meerkat's back. Carefully sew the open end of the tail to the meerkat's back using the seam to position the tail correctly.

FINISHING TOUCHES

Sew the eye patches on each side of the face using matching yarn. Embroider little stitches to form a circle in the centre of each patch using white yarn. Make a few black knots in the circles for the pupils. Embroider the nose and mouth using black yarn.

Cut four patches of fabric to make the foot and hand pads (see Templates). Bond fusible interfacing to the wrong side of the fabric. Neatly sew each pad onto the base of each foot and inside each hand. Use straight stitches in black yarn to add claws.

Baby Meerkat pattern

HEAD, BODY AND LEGS

Starting at head, cast on 7 sts in **yarn MC** using size 6 (4mm) knitting needles.

Row 1 Kfb 6 times, k1. (13 sts)
Row 2 P.
Row 3 [Kfb, k1, kfb] 4 times, k1. (21 sts)
Row 4 P.
Row 5 [Kfb, k3, kfb] 4 times, k1. (29 sts)
Row 6 P.
Row 7 K12, kfb 4 times, k13. (33 sts)
Row 8 P.
Row 9 K14, kfb 4 times, k15. (37 sts)
Row 10 P.
Row 11 K16, kfb 4 times, k17. (41 sts)
Row 12 P.
Row 13 K16, skpo twice, k1, k2tog twice, k16. (37 sts)
Row 14 P.
Row 15 K14, skpo twice, k1, k2tog twice, k14. (33 sts)
Row 16 P.
Row 17 K12, skpo twice, k1, k2tog twice, k12. (29 sts)
Row 18 P.
Row 19 [K2tog, k3, skpo] 4 times, k1. (21 sts)
Row 20 P.
Row 21 [K2tog, k1, skpo] 4 times, k1. (13 sts)
Row 22 P.

Cont for neck and body:
Row 23 K.
Row 24 P.
Row 25 [Kfb, k1, kfb] 4 times, k1. (21 sts)
Row 26 P.
Row 27 [Kfb, k3, kfb] 4 times, k1. (29 sts)
Row 28 P.
Row 29 [Kfb, k5, kfb] 4 times, k1. (37 sts)
Row 30 P.
Row 31 [Kfb, k7, kfb] 4 times, k1. (45 sts)
Row 32 P.
Cont in st st for 14 rows.
Row 47 [K2tog, k7, skpo] 4 times, k1. (37 sts)
Row 48 P.
Row 49 [K2tog, k5, skpo] 4 times, k1. (29 sts)
Row 50 P.
Row 51 [K2tog, k3, skpo] 4 times, k1. (21 sts)
Row 52 P.

Cont for right leg:
Row 53 K10, turn.
Row 54 P10.
Cont in st st for 30 rows.
Row 85 [K2tog] rep to end. (5 sts)
Thread yarn through rem sts and pull tight.

Cont for left leg, picking up rem 11 sts:
Row 53 K2tog, k9. (10 sts)
Row 54 P10.
Rep as for right leg.

EARS (MAKE 2)

Cast on 8 sts in **yarn A** using size 6 (4mm) knitting needles.
St st for 2 rows.
Row 3 [K2tog] rep to end. (4 sts)
Thread yarn through rem sts and pull tight.

TAIL

Cast on 12 sts in **yarn MC** using size 6 (4mm) knitting needles.
St st for 20 rows.
Row 21 [K1, k2tog] rep to end. (8 sts)
Row 22 P.
Row 23 K.
Row 24 P.
Thread yarn through rem sts and pull tight.

ARMS (MAKE 2)

Cast on 10 sts in **yarn MC** using size 6 (4mm) knitting needles.
St st for 30 rows.
Row 31 [K2tog] rep to end. (5 sts)
Row 32 P.
Thread yarn through rem sts and pull tight.

EYES (MAKE 2)

Cast on 4 sts in **yarn A** using size 6 (4mm) knitting needles.
Row 1 P.
Row 2 K1, kfb twice, k1. (6 sts)
Row 3 P.
Row 4 K1, k2tog twice, k1. (4 sts)
Row 5 P.
Bind off.

MAKING UP

Make up Baby Meerkat as for Mummy Meerkat.

Gerry Giraffe

Rating

Working with two colours and picking up stitches are the main techniques to master here

Some of the trees in Kenya grow very tall, which is why giraffes have long legs and necks to reach the very best leaves. Gerry looks so graceful as he stretches and arches his elegant neck.

Gerry is bound to keep you amused, especially keeping your tension even around his spots, working his stripy legs and adding character with his tail, mane and horns.

Yarn
Lightweight (DK) yarn:
1 x 1¾oz (50g) ball in ginger (**MC**)
1 x 1¾oz (50g) ball in brown (**A**)
Oddment of dark brown yarn for eyes, mouth and nose

Needles
Size 6 (4mm) knitting needles

Gauge
22 sts and 30 rows to 4in (10cm)

Finished size
16⅛in (41cm) tall

Gerry Giraffe can reach very high.
He stretches his long neck right up to the sky
He reaches up high for the juiciest leaves.
They're always on branches at the top of the trees

Don't worry if the gauge is not exact. It doesn't matter if your giraffe is a bit bigger or smaller than mine.

Gerry Giraffe pattern

HEAD, NECK AND BODY

Starting at nose, cast on 7 sts in **yarn MC** using size 6 (4mm) knitting needles.

Row 1 Kfb 6 times, k1. (13 sts)
Row 2 P.
Row 3 K3, kfb, k4, kfb, K4. (15 sts)
Row 4 P.
Row 5 K4, kfb, k4, kfb, k5. (17 sts)
Row 6 P.
Row 7 K5, kfb, k4, kfb, k6. (19 sts)
Row 8 P.
Row 9 K6, kfb, k4, kfb, k7. (21 sts)
Row 10 P.
Row 11 K2, [kfb, k4] 3 times, kfb, k3. (25 sts)
Row 12 P.
Row 13 K2, kfb, k6, kfb, k4, kfb, k6, kfb, k3. (29 sts)
Row 14 P.
Row 15 K2, kfb, k8, kfb, k4, kfb, k8, kfb, k3. (33 sts)
Row 16 P.
Row 17 K2, kfb, k10, kfb, k4, kfb, k10, kfb, k3. (37 sts)
Row 18 P.

Row 19 K2, kfb, k12, kfb, k4, kfb, k12, kfb, k3. (41 sts)
Row 20 P.
Row 21 K. Mark each end of this row.
Row 22 P.
Row 23 K2, skpo, k12, skpo, k5, k2tog, k12, k2tog, k2. (37 sts)
Row 24 P.
Row 25 K2, skpo, k10, skpo, k5, k2tog, k10, k2tog, k2. (33 sts)
Row 26 P.
Row 27 K2, skpo, k8, skpo, k5, k2tog, k8, k2tog, k2. (29 sts)
Row 28 P.
Row 29 K2, skpo, k6, skpo, k5, k2tog, k6, k2tog, k2. (25 sts)
Row 30 P.
Row 31 K2, skpo, k4, skpo, k5, k2tog, k4, k2tog, k2. (21 sts)
Row 32 P.
Row 33 [K2tog] rep to last st, k1. (11 sts)
Row 34 P.
Thread yarn through rem sts and pull tight.

Cont for neck:
Row 35 Pick up and knit 28 sts across back of head between markers. (14 sts from left shaping to centre and 14 sts from centre to right shaping).
Row 36 P.
Row 37 K. (28 sts)
Row 38 P.
Row 39 Knit with **yarn MC**, introducing **yarn A** for spot pattern as shown for row 39 on chart 1.
Cont pattern for 35 more rows, increasing at both ends of rows 45, 51, 57, 63 and 69 as shown on chart 1.

CHART 1

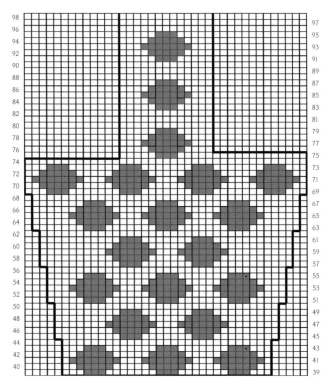

KEY
☐ yarn MC
▨ yarn A
▣ cut off brown yarn

Cont in pattern for giraffe's back, as shown on chart 1:

Row 75 K26, turn. Leave rem sts on stitch holder.

Row 76 Sl 1, p12, turn. (13 sts)
Leave rem sts on stitch holder.

Row 77 Sl 1, k12.
Cont in patt on these 13 sts for further 18 rows.

Row 96 P.

Row 97 K.

Row 98 P.
Cut yarn and put sts on stitch holder.

Cont for sides of giraffe's body in **yarn MC**:

Row 99 Slip 13 sts held at row 75 back onto needle, pick up and knit 13 sts from near side of giraffe's back, knit 13 sts held at row 98, pick up and knit 13 sts from far side of giraffe's back, knit 13 sts held at row 76. (65 sts)

Row 100 P.

Row 101 Cont pattern, working from chart 2 and increasing at both ends of row 101. (67 sts)
Cont for 17 rows, increasing at both ends of rows 107 and 113. (71sts)

Cont for underside of giraffe's body:

Row 119 Skpo twice, k27, skpo twice, k1, k2tog twice, k27, k2tog twice. (63 sts)

Row 120 P.

Row 121 Skpo twice, k23, skpo twice, k1, k2tog twice, k23, k2tog twice. (55 sts)

Row 122 P.

Row 123 Skpo twice, k19, skpo twice, k1, k2tog twice, k19, k2tog twice. (47 sts)

Row 124 P.
Bind off.

CHART 2

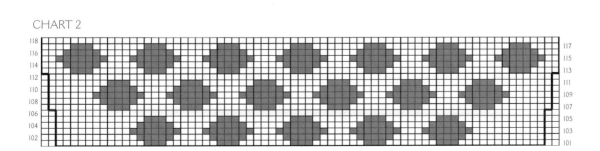

LEGS (MAKE 4)

Cast on 20 sts in **yarn MC** using size 6 (4mm) knitting needles.

St st for 34 rows, alternating **yarns MC** and A every 4 rows to make stripes.

Row 35 [K2tog] rep to end. (10 sts)

Row 36 P.

Thread yarn through rem sts and pull tight.

EARS (MAKE 2)

Cast on 10 sts in **yarn MC** using size 6 (4mm) knitting needles.

Row 1 K.

Row 2 P.

Row 3 K3, skpo, k2tog, k3. (8 sts)

Row 4 P.

Row 5 K2, skpo, k2tog, k2. (6 sts)

Row 6 P.

Row 7 K1, skpo, k2tog, k1. (4 sts)

Thread yarn through rem sts and pull tight.

TAIL

Cast on 12 sts in **yarn A** using size 6 (4mm) knitting needles.

St st for 20 rows.

Row 21 [K1, k2tog] rep to end. (8 sts)

Row 22 P.

Cont in st st for 6 rows.

Thread yarn through rem sts and pull tight.

HORNS (MAKE 2)

Cast on 5 sts in **yarn A** using size 6 (4mm) knitting needles.

St st for 4 rows.

Row 5 K1, kfb, kfb, k2. (7 sts)

Row 6 P.

Row 7 K.

Row 8 P.

Row 9 K2, kfb, kfb, k3. (9 sts)

Row 10 P.

Bind off.

MAKING UP

HEAD, BODY, TAIL AND LEGS
Sew up from the nose, under the neck and then along the body, leaving an opening for stuffing. Fill with stuffing and sew up the opening.

Sew up the back seam of the tail and stuff. Make a tassel using **yarn A** (see Techniques: Tassels) and sew it to the end of the tail. Sew the tail to the rear of the giraffe.

Sew up the legs and fill with stuffing. Sew them to the underside of the giraffe's body.

HORNS AND EARS
Sew up the back seams of the horns and fill with stuffing.

Sew the ears and horns onto the head using the shaping as a guide to position them.

MANE
Cut a strip of card ⅜in (1cm) wide and 12in (30cm) long.

Wrap **yarn A** around the width of the card. The more yarn you use the thicker the mane. Carefully stitch over and under the mane along one long edge and then back again so that every strand is secured.

Cut the mane along the other long edge so the mane is the same length on each side of the stitches.

Position the mane at the top of giraffe's head and down the back of his neck with the stitches in the centre. Secure the mane in place using back stitch.

FINISHING TOUCHES
Embroider the eyes, mouth and nose using dark brown yarn.

Cut four patches of fabric to make the footpads and another two for inner ears (see Templates). Bond fusible interfacing to the wrong side of the fabric. Neatly sew one pad onto the base of each foot and one inside each ear.

Gerry Giraffe saves the day

It was a baking hot day and Zoe the Zebra was
munching a clump of grass unaware of anything around
her. Lenny the Lion was lazing around, hidden in the
long grass. He opened one eye and spotted Zoe.

"Ah, lunch," he thought.

Lenny crept quietly through the grass towards the munching zebra.

Gerry Giraffe was nearby, reaching up to eat the leaves from the
top of the trees. He spotted the lion creeping towards the zebra.

"Oh no!" he thought, and he bellowed a warning
to Zoe at the top of his voice.

Zoe stopped and turned around to see the lion about
to pounce - but she was fast and speedily dashed off
across the plain. As she ran to her friends, she gave
a grateful nod to Gerry who smiled back at her.

Lenny the Lion

Use a simple rug-making knot to attach the mane and the knitting is straightforward

Lenny may laze around for most of the day, but he only has to roar to let all the animals in Angola know that he's the king of the jungle. He's very proud of his glorious, glossy mane and uses his favourite shampoo to make sure that it's always in beautiful condition.

Lenny's mane is so splendid because of its extravagant mohair content and the rest of his hair is lovely and silky. Choose your yarns with care to give him an equally regal appearance.

Yarn
Lightweight (DK) slubby merino/silk yarn:
1 x 3½oz (100g) ball in multi-coloured gold (**MC**)
Medium-weight (chunky) yarn:
1 x 1¾oz (50g) ball in amber (**A**)
Oddment of black yarn
Oddment of white yarn

Needles
Size 8 (5mm) knitting needles

Gauge
17 sts and 21 rows to 4in (10cm)

Finished size
8¼in (21cm) tall x 10⅛in (26cm) long (excluding tail)

Lenny the Lion lies under the trees.
He sleeps very soundly in the warm summer breeze.
Then lazily he wakes and stretches each paw.
He yawns and jumps up and gives a loud roar.

Don't worry if the gauge is not exact. It doesn't matter if your lion is a bit bigger or smaller than mine.

Lenny the Lion pattern

HEAD AND BODY
Starting at nose, cast on 6 sts in **yarn MC** using size 8 (5mm) knitting needles.
Row 1 Kfb 5 times, k1. (11 sts)
Row 2 P.
Row 3 Kfb 10 times, k1. (21 sts)
Row 4 P.
Row 5 K2, [kfb, k4] 3 times, kfb, k3. (25 sts)
Row 6 P.
Row 7 K2, kfb, k6, kfb, k4, kfb, k6, kfb, k3. (29 sts)
Row 8 P.
Row 9 K2, kfb, k8, kfb, k4, kfb, k8, kfb, k3. (33 sts)
Row 10 P.
Row 11 K2, kfb, k10, kfb, k4, kfb, k10, kfb, k3. (37 sts)
Row 12 P.
Row 13 K2, kfb, k12, kfb, k4, kfb, k12, kfb, k3. (41 sts)
Row 14 P.
Row 15 K2, kfb, k14, kfb, k4, kfb, k14, kfb, k3. (45 sts)
Row 16 P.
Row 17 K.
Row 18 P.
Row 19 K2, skpo, k14, skpo, k5, k2tog, k14, k2tog, k2. (41 sts)

Row 20 P.
Row 21 K2, skpo, k12, skpo, k5, k2tog, k12, k2tog, k2. (37 sts)
Row 22 P.
Row 23 K2, skpo, k10, skpo, k5, k2tog, k10, k2tog, k2. (33 sts)
Row 24 P.
Row 25 K2, skpo, k8, skpo, k5, k2tog, k8, k2tog, k2. (29 sts)
Row 26 P.
Row 27 K.
Row 28 P.

Cont for lion's body:
Row 29 K1, [kfb, k1] rep to end. (43 sts)
Row 30 P.
St st for 30 rows.
Row 61 K1, [k2tog, k1] rep to end. (29 sts)
Row 62 P.
Row 63 K1, [k2tog] rep to end. (15 sts)
Row 64 P.
Thread yarn through rem 15 sts and pull tight to form lion's bottom.

EARS (MAKE 2)
Cast on 3 sts in **yarn MC** using size 8 (5mm) knitting needles.
Row 1 Kfb twice, k1. (5 sts)
Row 2 P.
Row 3 K1, kfb twice, k2. (7 sts)
Row 4 P.
Row 5 K.
Row 6 P.
Bind off.

LEGS (MAKE 4)
Cast on 17 sts in **yarn MC** using size 8 (5mm) knitting needles.
St st for 12 rows.
Row 13 K7, kfb, kfb, k8. (19 sts)
Row 14 P.
Row 15 K8, kfb twice, k9. (21 sts)
Row 16 P.
Row 17 K9, kfb twice, k10. (23 sts)
Row 18 P.
Row 19 K2tog, k19, k2tog. (21 sts)
Row 20 P.
Row 21 [K1, k2tog] rep to end. (14 sts)
Row 22. P
Row 23. [K2tog] rep to end
Thread yarn through sts and pull tight.

TAIL
Cast on 10 sts in **yarn MC** using size 8 (5mm)
knitting needles.
St st for 24 rows.
Row 25 [K1, k2tog] rep to last st, k1. (7 sts)
Row 26 P.
Row 27 K.
Row 28 P.
Thread yarn through rem sts and pull tight.

MAKING UP

HEAD AND BODY
Sew from each end, leaving an opening. Fill with stuffing and sew up the opening.

EARS
Stitch the ears to each side of the lion's head using the shaping at the top of the head to position them.

LEGS
Sew from the heel to the top of each leg. Fill with stuffing.
Position the legs under the body and sew them securely in place.

TAIL
Neatly stitch the long sides together, stuffing the tail as you go.
Make a tassel from **yarn MC** (see Techniques: Tassels) and attach it to the end of the tail.
Sew the tail to the rear of the lion.

MANE
Sew running stitch all around the outer edge of the lion's face as a guideline for positioning the mane.
Fold lengths of **yarn A**, 12in (30cm) long, in half and half again. Using a large tapestry needle, thread the folded yarn and attach it to the mane guideline with a rug-making knot (see Techniques: Rug-making knot). Repeat all around the guideline to make the mane as fine or as thick as you wish.

FINISHING TOUCHES
Embroider lion's eyes in black yarn.
Embroider the lion's eyes in black and white yarn.
Embroider the nose and mouth using black yarn.
Add whiskers by securing in a few strands of black yarn to the muzzle and then separating the strands.
Cut four patches of fabric to make the footpads and another two for inner ears (see Templates). Bond fusible interfacing to the wrong side of the fabric.
Neatly sew one pad onto the base of each foot and one inside each ear.

Zoe the Zebra

Rating 🪁🪁

Picking up stitches to progress from one part of the toy to the next is the main challenge here

Zoe is very proud of her stripes as every zebra's markings are totally unique. They help her to hide in the long grass here in Ethiopia so there's less chance of her becoming anyone's lunch!

Attach plenty of yarn to make Zoe's exuberant mane. The combination of black and white looks very distinguished, but you can add a bit of colour with your choice of fabric for Zoe's ears and feet.

Yarn
Lightweight (DK) yarn
1 x 1¾oz (50g) ball in black (**MC**)
1 x 1¾oz (50g) ball in white (**A**)

Needles
Size 6 (4mm) knitting needles
Size G/6 (4mm) crochet hook

Gauge
22 sts and 30 rows to 4in (10cm)

Finished sizes
11⅜in (29cm) tall x 9in (23cm) long

Zoe the Zebra runs very fast.
She stops to nibble the long green grass.
She spots a lion lurking while taking a munch.
'I don't fancy being that greedy lion's lunch.'

Don't worry if the
gauge is not exact. It
doesn't matter if your
zebra is a bit bigger or
smaller than mine.

Zoe the Zebra pattern

HEAD, NECK AND BODY
Starting at nose, cast on 15 sts in waste yarn using size
G/6 (4mm) knitting needles.
Knit 4 rows. (Later you will unravel these rows and
thread **yarn A** through sts to close).

Change to **yarn A**, leaving a 4in (10cm) end of yarn.
Row 1 [K4, kfb] twice, k5. (17 sts)
Row 2 P.
Row 3 K5, kfb, k4, kfb, k6. (19 sts)
Row 4 P.
Change to **yarn MC**.
Row 5 K6, kfb, k4, kfb, k7. (21 sts)
Row 6 P.
Row 7 K2, [kfb, k4] 3 times, kfb, k3. (25 sts)
Row 8 P.
Change to **yarn A**.
Row 9 K2, kfb, k6, kfb, k4, kfb, k6, kfb, k3. (29 sts)
Row 10 P.
Row 11 K2, kfb, k8, kfb, k4, kfb, k8, kfb, k3. (33 sts)
Row 12 P.
Change to **yarn MC**.
Row 13 K2, kfb, k10, kfb, k4, kfb, k10, kfb, k3. (37 sts)
Row 14 P.
Row 15 K2, kfb, k12, kfb, k4, kfb, k12, kfb, k3. (41 sts)
Row 16 P.
Change to **yarn A**.
Row 17 K2, kfb, k14, kfb, k4, kfb, k14, kfb, k3. (45 sts)
Row 18 P.
Row 19 K2, kfb, k16, kfb, k4, kfb, k16, kfb, k3. (49 sts)
Row 20 P. Mark each end of this row.
Change to **yarn MC**.
Row 21 K.
Row 22 P.
Row 23 K.
Row 24 P.
Change to **yarn A**.
Row 25 K2, skpo, k16, skpo, k5, k2tog, k16, k2tog,
k2. (45 sts)
Row 26 P.
Row 27 K2, skpo, k14, skpo, k5, k2tog, k14, k2tog,
k2. (41 sts)
Row 28 P.
Change to **yarn MC**.

Row 29 K2, skpo, k12, skpo, k5, k2tog, k12, k2tog,
k2. (37 sts)
Row 30 P.
Row 31 K2, skpo, k10, skpo, k5, k2tog, k10, k2tog, k2.
(33 sts)
Row 32 P.
Change to **yarn A**.
Row 33 K2, skpo, k8, skpo, k5, k2tog, k8, k2tog, k2.
(29 sts)
Row 34 P.
Row 35 K2, skpo, k6, skpo, k5, k2tog, k6, k2tog, k2.
(25 sts)
Row 36 P.
Change to **yarn MC**.
Row 37 K2, skpo, k4, skpo, k5, k2tog, k4, k2tog, k2.
(21 sts)
Row 38 P.
Row 39 [K2tog] rep to last st, k1. (11 sts)
Row 40 P.
Thread yarn through rem sts and pull tight.

Cont for neck in **yarn MC**:
Row 41 Pick up and knit 32 sts across back bottom
edges of head between markers (16 sts from left
shaping to the centre and 16 sts from centre to right
shaping).
Row 42 P.
Row 43 Kfb, k29, kfb, k1. (34 sts)
Row 44 P.
Change to **yarn A**.
Row 45 Kfb, k31, kfb, k1. (36 sts)
Row 46 P.
Row 47 K.
Row 48 P.

Cont for zebra's back:
Change to **yarn MC**.
Row 49 K24, turn. Leave rem sts on stitch holder.
Row 50 Sl 1, p11, turn. (12 sts)
Leave rem sts on stitch holder.
Row 51 Sl 1, k11.
Row 52 Sl 1, p11.
Change to **yarn A**.
Cont on 12 sts for 28 more rows, changing stripes
every 4 rows. Cut yarn and leave sts on stitch holder.

Cont for sides of zebra's body:
Change to **yarn MC**.
Row 81 Slip 12 sts left on stitch holder at row 50 onto needle, rejoin **yarn MC** at inner edge, pick up and knit 23 sts from near side of zebra's back, knit 12 sts held at row 80, pick up and knit 23 sts from far side of zebra's back, knit 12 sts held at the end of row 49. (82 sts)
Row 82 P.
Row 83 K.
Row 84 P.
Change to **yarn A**.
Row 85 Kfb, k79, kfb, k1. (84 sts)
Row 86 P.
Row 87 K.
Row 88 P.
Change to **yarn MC**.
Row 89 Kfb, k81, kfb, k1. (86 sts)
Row 90 P.
Row 91 K.
Row 92 P.
Change to **yarn A**.
Row 93 Kfb, k83, kfb, k1. (88 sts)
Row 94 P.
Row 95 K.
Row 96 P.

Cont for underside of zebra's body:
Change to **yarn MC**.
Row 97 Skpo twice, k36, skpo twice, k2tog twice, k36, k2tog twice. (80 sts)
Row 98 P.
Row 99 Skpo twice, k32, skpo twice, k2tog twice, k32, k2tog twice. (72 sts)
Row 100 P.
Change to **yarn A**.
Row 101 Skpo twice, k28, skpo twice, k2tog twice, k28, k2tog twice. (64 sts)
Row 102 P.
Row 103 Skpo twice, k24, skpo twice, k2tog twice, k24, k2tog twice. (56 sts)
Row 104 P.
Change to **yarn MC**.
Row 105 Skpo twice, k20, skpo twice, k2tog twice, k20, k2tog twice. (48 sts)
Row 106 P.
Bind off.

LEGS (MAKE 4)

Cast on 20 sts in **yarn MC** using size 6 (4mm) knitting needle.

St st for 28 rows, alternating **yarn MC** to **yarn A** every 4 rows.

Cont in **yarn MC**.

Row 29 [K2tog] rep to end. (10 sts)

Row 30 P.

Thread yarn through rem sts and pull tight.

EARS (MAKE 2)

Cast on 12 sts in **yarn MC** using size 6 (4mm) knitting needle.

Row 1 K.

Row 2 P.

Row 3 K4, skpo, k2tog, k4. (10 sts)

Row 4 P.

Row 5 K3, skpo, k2tog, k3. (8 sts)

Row 6 P.

Row 7 K2, skpo, k2tog, k2. (6 sts)

Row 8 P.

Row 9 K1, skpo, k2tog, k1. (4 sts)

Thread yarn through rem sts and pull tight.

TAIL

Crochet a chain (see Techniques: Crochet chains) 2⅜in (6cm) long using six strands of **yarn MC**, two strands of **yarn A** and size G/6 (4mm) crochet hook. Alternatively, plait four strands of **yarn MC** and two strands of **yarn A** together to make the tail.

Leave a further 2in (5cm) end for the end of the tail. Tie a knot at the end of the chain stitch and, using a sewing needle, fray out the yarn ends at the end of the tail to give a frizzy appearance. Add more threads to the end of the tail if you want a bigger look.

MAKING UP

HEAD, NECK AND BODY

Thread a length of **yarn A** through the stitches in the same colour at the nose. Unravel the stitches in waste yarn. Draw up the remaining stitches on yarn A and fasten off securely.

Sew up from the nose, under the neck and then along the body, leaving an opening for stuffing. Fill with stuffing and sew up the opening.

Sew the ears onto each side of the head.

Sew up the legs and fill with stuffing. Sew them underneath of the body.

Sew the tail securely.

MANE

Cut a strip of card 1½in (4cm) wide and 4¾in (12cm) long.

Wrap **yarn MC** and **yarn A** around the width of the card. The more yarn you use, the thicker the mane. Carefully stitch over and under the mane along one long edge and then back again so that every strand is secured.

Cut the mane along the long edge so the mane is the same length on each side of the stitches.

Position the mane at the top of the zebra's head and down the back of her neck with the stitches in the centre. Secure the mane using back stitch.

FINISHING TOUCHES

Embroider eyes, mouth and nose using **yarn MC**. Cut four patches of fabric to make the footpads and another two for inner ears (see Templates). Bond fusible interfacing to the wrong side of the fabric. Neatly sew one pad onto the base of each foot and one inside each ear.

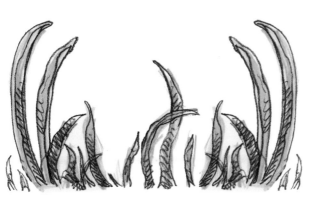

Patsy Polar Bear meets Rob the Reindeer

It was snowing hard. Big flakes of snow were dropping out of the sky. Patsy Polar Bear was walking across the frozen snow looking for somewhere sheltered to sleep for the night.

In the far distance she spotted something brown. Was it a tree? She walked a bit closer and saw what she thought were branches. The snow continued to float down from the sky while Patsy walked towards the brown object.

"What could it be?" she wondered.

Then slowly the object moved. It waved its branches and grew up from the ground. This wasn't a tree. It was Rob the Reindeer. He looked at Patsy and galloped off to join his herd.

Patsy Polar Bear continued on her way and found a quiet and warm spot to settle down and fall asleep.

Patsy Polar Bear

Rating

These simple shapes are knitted separately and sewn together

Polar bears are the largest mammals living on Greenland and Patsy is one of the most beautiful. When she wakes from hibernation, she likes nothing better than a good stretch and a roll in the snows of spring.

Patsy's luxurious thick coat is created with cream-coloured yarn, but you could make an Asiatic Black Bear or American Grizzly by choosing different colours. This simply pattern and easy shaping are perfect for any type of bear.

Yarn
Lightweight (DK) yarn:
1 x 1¾oz (50g) ball in cream (**MC**)
Oddment of black yarn

Needles
Size 6 (4mm) knitting needles

Gauge
22 sts and 30 rows to 4in (10cm)

Finished sizes
6¼in (16cm) tall x 9½in (24cm) long

Patsy's coat is warm and white.
She lives in the Arctic where it's cold day and night.
She digs herself into a hole in the snow.
And patiently waits for the blizzard to go.

Patsy the Polar Bear pattern

HEAD AND BODY

Starting at nose, cast on 7 sts in **yarn MC** using size 6 (4mm) knitting needles.

Row 1 Kfb, k1, kfb twice, k1, kfb, k1. (11 sts)
Row 2 P.
Row 3 Kfb, k8, kfb, k1. (13 sts)
Row 4 P.
Row 5 Kfb, k4, kfb twice, k4, kfb, k1. (17 sts)
Row 6 P.
Row 7 Kfb, k14, kfb, k1. (19 sts)
Row 8 P.
Row 9 Kfb, k7, kfb twice, k7, kfb, k1. (23 sts)
Row 10 P.
Row 11 Kfb, k20, kfb, k1. (25 sts)
Row 12 P.
Row 13 Kfb, k10, kfb twice, k10, kfb, k1. (29 sts)
Row 14 P.
Row 15 Kfb, k26, kfb, k1. (31 sts)
Row 16 P.
Row 17 Kfb, k13, kfb twice, k13, kfb, k1. (35 sts)
Row 18 P.
Row 19 Kfb, k32, kfb, k1. (37 sts)
Row 20 P.
Row 21 Kfb, k16, kfb twice, k16, kfb, k1. (41 sts)
Row 22 P.
Row 23 Kfb, k38, kfb, k1. (43 sts)
Row 24 P.
Row 25 Kfb, k19, kfb twice, k19, kfb, k1. (47 sts)
Row 26 P.
Cont in st st for 40 rows.
Row 67 [K2tog] rep to last st, k1. (24 sts)
Row 68 P.
Row 69 [K2tog] rep to end. (12 sts)
Thread yarn through rem sts and pull tight to form bear's bottom.

EARS (MAKE 2)

Cast on 6 sts in **yarn MC** using size 6 (4mm) knitting needles.

St st for 4 rows.

Row 5 K2tog 3 times. (3 sts)

Row 6 P.

Row 7 Kfb 3 times. (6 sts)

Row 8 P.

Row 9 K.

Row 10 P.

Row 11 K.

Bind off.

LEGS (MAKE 4)

Cast on 5 sts in **yarn MC** using size 6 (4mm) knitting needles.

Row 1 Kfb 5 times. (10 sts)

Row 2 P.

Row 3 Kfb 10 times. (20 sts)

Row 4 P.

Row 5 K7, kfb 6 times, k7. (26 sts)

Row 6 P.

Cont in st st for 4 rows.

Row 11 K7, k2tog 6 times, k7. (20 sts)

Row 12 P.

Cont in st st for 10 rows.

Bind off.

TAIL

Cast on 4 sts in **yarn MC** using size 6 (4mm) knitting needles.

St st for 4 rows.

Row 5 K2tog twice. (2 sts)

Row 6 P.

Row 7 K2tog. (1 st)

Thread yarn through rem st and pull tight.

MAKING UP

HEAD AND BODY

Sew from each end, leaving an opening for stuffing. Fill with stuffing and sew up the opening.

EARS

Fold each ear in half, right sides out, and sew up the back seam. Sew around the edge to form a double thickness.

Stitch the ears to each side of the bear's head using the shaping at the top of the head to position them.

LEGS

Sew from the heel to the top of each leg. Fill with stuffing.

Position the legs under the body and sew them on securely.

TAIL

Fold in half and stitch the long edges together. Fill with stuffing.

Sew the tail to the rear of the bear.

FINISHING TOUCHES

Embroider the eyes, nose and mouth using black yarn. Cut four patches of fabric to make the footpads and another two for inner ears (see Templates). Bond fusible interfacing to the wrong side of the fabric. Neatly sew one pad onto the base of each foot and one inside each ear.

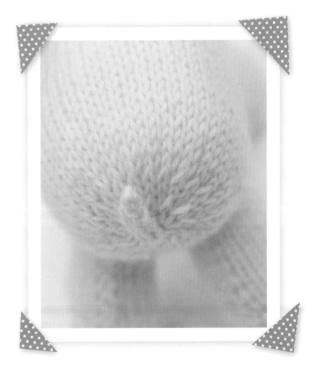

Rob the Reindeer

Rating ⟨⟨⟨⟩⟩⟩ ⟨⟨⟨⟩⟩⟩

You will need to pick up stitches to work from the head to the neck

When he's not pulling Santa's sleigh, Rob is racing around the snowy landscapes of Norway. His big red nose and tinkling bell make sure that he never gets lost – a true leader of herds of reindeer.

You can make Rob as majestic as you wish by building up his antlers, embellishing his collar and making him a dazzling pompom nose. Then he'll really look like the king of the icy forests and steppes.

Yarn
Medium-weight (Aran) yarn:
2 x 1¾oz (50g) ball in brown (**MC**)
Lightweight (DK) yarn:
1 x 1¾oz (50g) ball in taupe (**A**)
Oddments of green, red, yellow, black and white yarn

Needles
Size 8 (5mm) knitting needles
Size 6 (4mm) knitting needles

Gauge
18 sts and 20 rows to 4in (10cm)

Finished size
15in (38cm) tall x 13½in (34cm) long

Rob the Reindeer has a coat that is thick.
He has long, strong legs and hooves that can kick.
His antlers are huge and not very light,
and his big red nose is incredibly bright.

Don't worry if the gauge is not exact. It doesn't matter if your reindeer is a bit bigger or smaller than mine. If you want to make the antlers more solid, knit them on small sized needles with lots of strands of yarn. Cast on more stitches if you want longer antler branches.

Rob the Reindeer
pattern

HEAD, NECK AND BODY

Starting at nose, cast on 7 sts in **yarn MC** using size 8 (5mm) knitting needles.

Row 1 Kfb 6 times, k1. (13 sts)
Row 2 P.
Row 3 K3, kfb, k4, kfb, k4. (15 sts)
Row 4 P.
Row 5 K4, kfb, k4, kfb, k5. (17 sts)
Row 6 P.
Row 7 K5, kfb, k4, kfb, k6. (19 sts)
Row 8 P.
Row 9 K6, kfb, k4, kfb, k7. (21 sts)
Row 10 P.
Row 11 K2, [kfb, k4] 3 times, kfb, k3. (25 sts)
Row 12 P.
Row 13 K2, kfb, k6, kfb, k4, kfb, k6, kfb, k3. (29 sts)
Row 14 P.
Row 15 K2, kfb, k8, kfb, k4, kfb, k8, kfb, k3. (33 sts)
Row 16 P.
Row 17 K2, kfb, k10, kfb, k4, kfb, k10, kfb, k3. (37 sts)
Row 18 P.
Row 19 K2, kfb, k12, kfb, k4, kfb, k12, kfb, k3. (41 sts)
Row 20 P.
Row 21 K. (Mark each end of this row.)
Row 22 P.
Row 23 K2, skpo, k12, skpo, k5, k2tog, k12, k2tog, k2. (37 sts)
Row 24 P.

Row 25 K2, skpo, k10, skpo, k5, k2tog, k10, k2tog, k2. (33 sts)
Row 26 P.
Row 27 K2, skpo, k8, skpo, k5, k2tog, k8, k2tog, k2. (29 sts)
Row 28 P.
Row 29 K2, skpo, k6, skpo, k5, k2tog, k6, k2tog, k2. (25 sts)
Row 30 P.
Row 31 K2, skpo, k4, skpo, k5, k2tog, k4, k2tog, k2.(21 sts)
Row 32 P.
Row 33 [K2tog] rep to last st, k1. (11 sts)
Row 34 P.
Thread yarn through rem sts and pull tight.
Cont for neck:
Row 35 Using the shaping of reindeer's head pick up, on size 8 (5mm) knitting needles and in **yarn MC**, and knit 28 sts across the back of the head between markers (14 sts from left shaping to the centre and 14 sts from centre to right shaping).
Row 36 P.
Row 37 Kfb, k25, kfb, k1. (30 sts)
Row 38 P.
Row 39 Kfb, k27, kfb, k1. (32 sts)
Row 40 P.
Row 41 K.
Row 42 P.

Cont for reindeer's back:
Row 43 K21, turn. Leave rem sts on stitch holder.
Row 44 Sl 1, p9, turn. Leave rem sts on stitch holder.
Row 45 Sl 1, k9.
Row 46 Sl 1, p9.
Cont on these 10 sts for 24 more rows. Cut yarn and leave sts on stitch holder.
Cont for sides of reindeer's body in **yarn MC** using size 8 (5mm knitting needles):
Row 71 Slip 11 sts left on stitch holder at row 44 onto needle, rejoin **yarn MC** at inner edge, pick up and knit 16 sts from near side of reindeer's back, knit 10 sts held at row 70, pick up and knit 16 sts from far side of reindeer's back, knit 11 sts held at row 43. (64 sts)

Row 72 P.
Row 73 Kfb, k61, kfb, k1. (66 sts)
Row 74 P.
Row 75 K.
Row 76 P.
Row 77 Kfb, k63, kfb, k1. (68 sts)
Row 78 P.
Row 79 K.
Row 80 P.
Row 81 Kfb, k65, kfb, k1. (70 sts)
Row 82 P.
Row 83 K.
Row 84 P.

Cont for underside of reindeer's body:
Row 85 Skpo twice, k27, skpo twice, k2tog twice, k27, k2tog twice. (62 sts)
Row 86 P.
Row 87 Skpo twice, k23, skpo twice, k2tog twice, k23, k2tog twice. (54 sts)
Row 88 P.
Row 89 Skpo twice, k19, skpo twice, k2tog twice, k19, k2tog twice. (46 sts)
Row 90 P.
Bind off.

LEGS (MAKE 4)
Cast on 20 sts in **yarn MC** using size 10 (6mm) knitting needles.
Cont in st st for 22 rows.
Row 23 [K2tog] rep to end. (10 sts)
Row 24 P.
Thread yarn through rem sts and pull tight.

EARS (MAKE 2)
Cast on 10 sts in **yarn MC** using size 10 (6mm) knitting needles.
Row 1 K.
Row 2 P.
Row 3 K3, skpo, k2tog, k3. (8 sts)
Row 4 P.
Row 5 K2, skpo, (4 sts), k2tog, k2. (6 sts)
Row 6 P.
Row 7 K1, skpo.k2tog, k1.
Thread yarn through rem sts and pull tight.

TAIL
Cast on 10 sts in **yarn MC** using size 10 (6mm) knitting needles.
Row 1 K.
Row 2 P.
Row 3 K.
Row 4 P.
Row 5 [K1, k2tog] to last st, k1. (7 sts)
Row 6 P.
Row 7 K.
Row 8 P.
Row 9 [K2tog] to last st, k1. (4 sts)
Row 10 P.
Thread yarn through rem sts and pull tight.

MAIN ANTLERS (MAKE 2)
Cast on 16 sts in four strands of **yarn A** using size 6 (4mm) knitting needles and leaving an end of approx 4in (10cm) to sew antlers to reindeer's head later.
Bind off.

ANTLER BRANCHES (MAKE 4)
Cast on 6 sts in four strands of **yarn A** using size 6 (4mm) knitting needles.
Bind off. Cut yarn, leaving an end of approx 4in (10cm) for attaching branches to antlers later.

COLLAR
Cast on 5 sts in green using size 10 (6mm) knitting needles.
Knit 50 rows.
Bind off.

BELL
Cast on 10 sts in yellow using size 10 (6mm) knitting needles.
Row 1 (WS) K (to form a ridge).
Row 2 K.
Row 3 P.
Row 4 K.
Row 5 P1, p2tog, p1, p2tog, p1, p2tog, p1. (7 sts)
Row 6 K.
Row 7 [P2tog] 3 times, p1. (4 sts)
Row 8 K.
Thread yarn through rem sts and pull tight.

MAKING UP

HEAD, BODY, TAIL AND LEGS
Sew up from the nose, under the neck and then along the body, leaving an opening for stuffing. Fill with stuffing and sew up the opening.
Sew up the back seam of the tail and stuff. Stitch the tail to the rear of the reindeer.
Sew up the legs and fill with stuffing. Sew them to the underside of the reindeer's body.

EARS AND ANTLERS
Stitch one ear to each side of the reindeer's head using the shaping as a guide to position them.
Using the attached ends of yarn, sew two antler branches to each main antler. Then sew the base of each main antler to the top of the head between the ears.

COLLAR
Wrap the collar around the reindeer's neck and sew the ends together.
Embroider small dots for extra detail, using red yarn.

BELL
Sew down the side of the bell.
Thread a long strand of yellow yarn through the top of the bell and loop it around the collar. You could knot the strand of yarn several times to give it more texture.

NOSE
Make a pompom (see Templates), using red yarn. Attach it to the top of the reindeer's nose.

FINISHING TOUCHES
Embroider the eyes and mouth using black yarn. Outline the eyes in white.
Cut four patches of fabric to make the footpads (see Templates). Bond fusible interfacing to the wrong side of the fabric. Neatly sew each pad onto the base of each foot.

Techniques

I want all knitters to be able to experience the fun and pleasure of making their own special knitted toys, so I've included projects simple enough for beginners and more ambitious projects for knitters ready for more of a challenge. If you are just learning, or you need to brush up your skills, I've included basic techniques such as casting on, making the knit and purl stitches, and binding off. All of the toys require shaping of some sort and I have included the methods I use for increasing and decreasing. Quite a few of the toys also feature colourwork, so knitting stripes and the intarsia and Fair Isle techniques are described. Making up the toys and embellishing them with their finishing touches will make all the difference to how your toys turn out. Take care over these details and you'll have toys to treasure for a lifetime!

Abbreviations

All knitting patterns use abbreviations to save time and space when writing out the instructions. These may seem a bit daunting if you are not familiar with the terms, but you will quickly pick up the language. Below is a list of all the abbreviations used in the patterns for this book.

approx approximately

cm(s) centimetre(s)

cont continue

DK double knitting

g gram(s)

in(s) inch(es)

k knit

k2tog knit the next two stitches together (decrease by one stitch)

kfb knit forward and back into the same stitch (increase by one stitch)

m metre(s)

MC main colour

mm millimetre(s)

oz ounce(s)

p purl

p2tog purl the next two stitches together (decrease by one stitch)

patt pattern

psso pass the slipped stitch over (decrease by one stitch)

rem remaining

rep repeat

skpo slip one, knit one, pass the slipped stitch over (decrease by one stitch)

sl1 slip one stitch

st(s) stitch(es)

st st stockinette stitch (stocking stitch)

tog together

yd yard(s)

Casting on

I wanted to make the patterns in this book appealing to beginner knitters as well as to those with more experience. If you are new to knitting, or could do with a reminder of some of the main techniques, I have included instructions for some of the basics you will need to make the toys. Any project starts with casting on the stitches - this means getting the initial stitches onto the knitting needles.

There are quite a few different ways of casting on, and you may have your own favourite method. However, the knitting-on method is a simple and versatile technique.

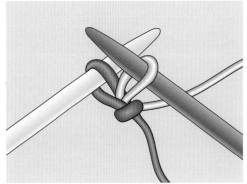

1 Make a slipknot in the working end of your yarn and place it on the left-hand needle. Insert your right-hand needle into the loop of the knot and wrap the yarn around the tip of the needle, from back to front.

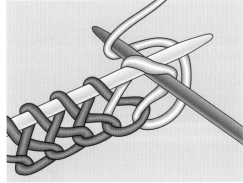

2 Slide the tip of the right-hand needle down to catch this new loop of yarn.

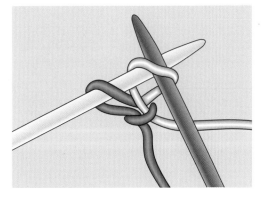

3 Place the new loop on the left-hand needle.

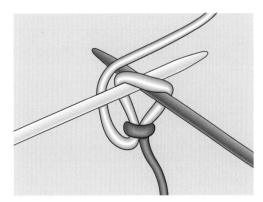

4 Repeat this process until you have cast on as many stitches as the project requires.

The knit and purl stitches

The knit stitch and the purl stitch are the two most basic stitches in knitting, but you will get a long way just knowing these two. Here is a popular way, sometimes called the English method, of making these stitches. An alternative, the Continental method, is given on the following two pages. The toys are mostly knitted in stockinette stitch (sometimes called stocking stitch by European knitters), which involves knitting one row and purling the next row.

The knit stitch

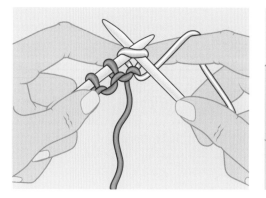

1 The working stitches will be on the left-hand needle. Take the right-hand needle and insert the tip from right to left into the first loop on the left-hand needle.

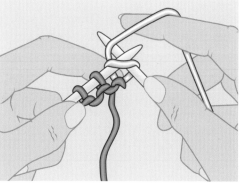

2 Wrap the yarn from back to front around the tip of the right-hand needle.

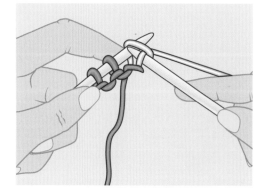

3 Slide the needle down to catch this new loop of yarn. Slip the loop off the left-hand needle and onto the right-hand needle. This is your first stitch. Repeat the process until all the stitches have been knitted off the left-hand needle onto the right-hand one.

The purl stitch

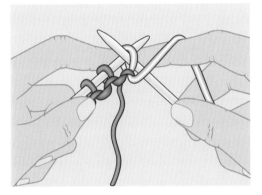

1 The working stitches will be on your left-hand needle.

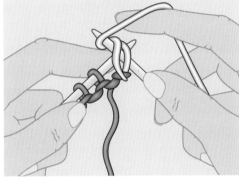

2 Wrap the yarn counterclockwise around the tip of the right-hand needle.

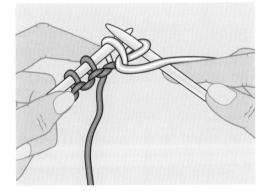

3 Use the tip of the right-hand needle to pick up the new loop of yarn. Slide the loop off the left-hand needle and onto the right-hand needle. This is your first stitch. Repeat the process until all the stitches have been knitted off the left-hand needle onto the right-hand one.

The knit stitch

Continental method *(yarn in the left hand)*
In this method the right-hand needle moves to catch the yarn; the yarn is held at the back of the work (the side facing away from you) and is released by the index finger of the left hand. This knit stitch is made up of four steps.

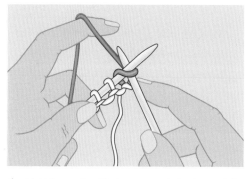

1 Hold the needle with the cast on stitches in your left hand and the yarn over your left index finger. Insert the right-hand needle into the front of the stitch from left to right.

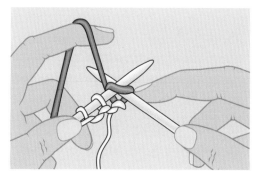

2 Move the right-hand needle down and across the back of the yarn.

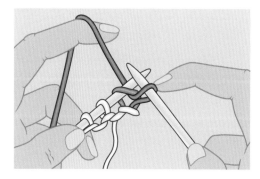

3 Pull the new loop on the right-hand needle through the stitch on the left-hand needle, using the right index finger to hold the new loop if needed.

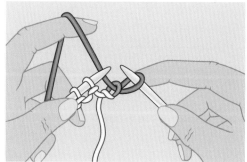

4 Slip the stitch off the left-hand needle. One knit stitch is completed.

The purl stitch

Continental method *(yarn in the left hand)*
In purl stitch the yarn is held at the front of the work (the side facing you) and is made up of four steps.

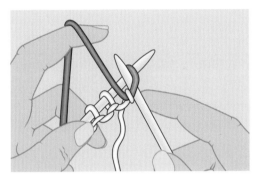

1 Hold the needle with the cast on stitches in your left hand, and insert the right-hand needle into the front of the stitch from right to left, keeping the yarn at the front of the work. .

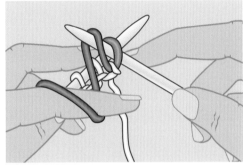

2 Move the right-hand needle from right to left behind the yarn and then from left to right in front of the yarn. Pull your left index finger down in front of the work to keep the yarn taut.

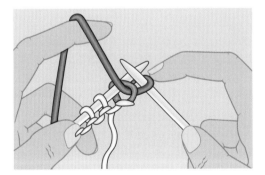

3 Pull the new loop on the right-hand needle through the stitch on the left-hand needle, using the right index finger to hold the new loop if needed.

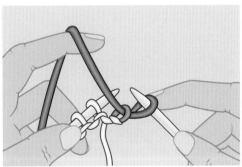

4 Slip the stitch off the left-hand needle. Return the left index finger to its position above the needle. One stitch is completed

Basic stitch patterns

I have used basic stitch patterns to make the knitted toys in this book; they are mostly knitted in stockinette stitch, with a few details knitted in garter stitch.

Stockinette stitch

Stockinette stitch (also referred to as stocking stitch by Europeans) is the main knitted fabric and the one that features most often in knitted designs. It is created by knitting one row and purling the next row. The knitted side forms the 'right side' or the outer side; the purl side forms the 'wrong side', or the inside.

Garter stitch

Garter stitch is created by knitting every row. This creates quite a dense fabric that looks the same on both sides. It was very useful for Ed's clothes. Bands of garter stitch on his shorts and coat give the bottom edges some substance and the same treatment around the top edges of his socks help to keep them up!

Gauge

On the band or sleeve of every ball of yarn there is information on the gauge (what European knitters call 'tension') of the yarn. This tells you how many stitches and rows you should aim to achieve over 4in (10cm) square. The gauge will differ depending on the size of the needles you use and the thickness of the yarn. However, we all knit differently. Some people are naturally loose knitters and others knit more tightly. The beauty about toys is that the gauge doesn't really matter in most cases. If your toy is a little bit bigger or smaller than mine, who's to know! Knitting is fun and should be for everyone. The only exception in this book is with Ed the Explorer; you should try to achieve the suggested gauge for both Ed and his clothes, or you may find that the clothes don't fit him properly.

Binding off

The last stage of knitting the toys will be binding off. Then you can move onto the making up!

Standard bind-off

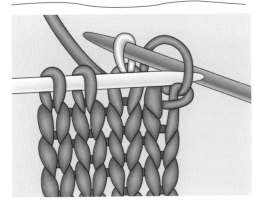

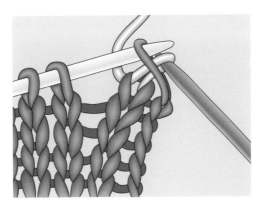

1 Work the first stitch on the left-hand needle as if making a usual knit stitch. Then knit the second stitch. Insert the left-hand needle into the first stitch on the right-hand needle.

2 Pass this over the second loop on the right-hand needle and drop it off the needle. This makes the first bound-off stitch. To continue, knit the next stitch. Use your left-hand needle to pass the first stitch over the second stitch and drop it off the needle. Carry on until all the stitches in the row have been bound off.

Shaping

I am not a fan of knitting lots of components for each toy and then having to sew them up at the end. I like to see the toy develop as it is being knitted. Therefore, my patterns have been created with shaping (increasing and decreasing stitches). This gives you a three-dimensional effect without all the sewing. I have used several shaping techniques, which are explained below.

Increasing stitches

Increasing stitches is where you make a stitch.

KFB (KNIT INTO THE FRONT AND BACK)

Knit along the row until you reach the area you want to increase. Knit into the front of the stitch on the left-hand needle. Instead of removing it from the needle (as with a normal knitted stitch), knit into it again through the back loop. Then slip the original stitch off the left-hand needle.

Decreasing stitches

Decreasing stitches is where you lose a stitch. This can be achieved in several ways.

SKPO (SLIP ONE, KNIT ONE, PASS THE SLIPPED STITCH OVER)

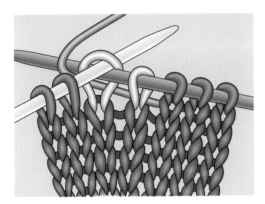
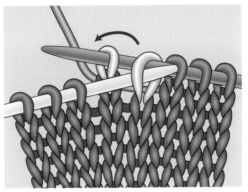

1 Knit along the row until you reach the area you want to decrease. Slip the stitch (unknitted) onto the right-hand needle. Knit the next stitch.

2 Lift the slipped stitch over the knitted stitch and off the needle. This decreases by one stitch.

K2TOG (KNIT TWO STITCHES TOGETHER)

Knit along the row until you reach the area you want to decrease. Knit through the next two stitches as though they were one stitch. This decreases by one stitch.

Colourwork

There are various ways to knit designs using two or more colours: stripes, Fair Isle and intarsia. Fair Isle is used to produce small-scale, intricate colour patterns, often using repeated motifs. You usually use two colours of yarn in a single row of knitting, and these yarns are stranded (carried) across the row at the back of the work. Intarsia is used to create larger chunks or blocks of colour. You will need a separate ball of yarn for each colour and you will often have to change colours in the middle of a row.

Stripes

Knitting stripes is the easiest way to add colour to a toy. Stripes are used for Zoe the Zebra, but could easily be incorporated into any toy. It is best to keep the colour changes to an even number over just a few rows so that you can carry the yarn up the same side of the project as you go.

When you come to the end of one stripe, don't cut the yarn. Instead, create a neater finish by just starting to knit with the second colour. The next time you get to that side and want to change colours, pick up the first colour, wrap the yarn you're working with around it and continue knitting.

Intarsia

Intarsia knitting is used for designs where there are big blocks of colour. Separate balls of wool are used for each block; unlike Fair Isle, no floats (or strands) of yarn are created at the back of the work. Intarsia colourwork is used in quite a few of the designs: Penny the Panda, Terry Tiger, Polly the Parrot and Monkey Mike.

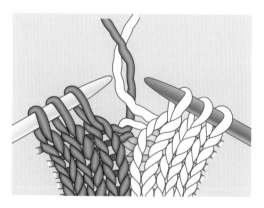

Knit along the row until the new colour is needed. Drop the first colour and pick up the second colour underneath the first colour, crossing the two colours over before knitting the next stitch in the second colour. The crossing of the stitches ensures that no holes are created between colours.

Fair Isle

I have used the Fair Isle technique on Gerry Giraffe's neck and body.

In Fair Isle knitting, each ball of wool is kept in action; you never cut the wool between stitches. Floats or strands are created as you work; these are horizontal strands of yarn that lie on the reverse side of the knitted fabric.

Knit along the row in your first colour until you come to the stitch where you need to change colour. To knit a stitch in your second colour, put the right-hand needle through the next stitch, pulling the new coloured yarn through as the stitch. This will create a float. It is important not to pull the stitches too tightly when working on the next stitch or the knitted fabric will be distorted.

The best way to work Fair Isle is to hold one colour yarn in your right hand (usually the background colour) and the other colour yarn in your left hand.

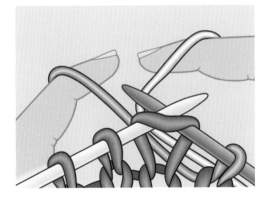

1 When knitting with the right-hand colour, keep the left-hand colour below the needle and out of the way of the working yarn.

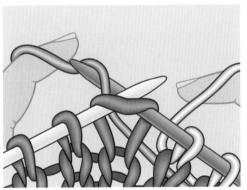

2 When knitting with the left-hand colour, keep the right-hand colour above the needle.

FAIR ISLE CHARTS
Fair Isle patterns are usually shown on a chart because it makes it easier to see how the pattern should look. You start at the bottom of the chart and work up. Each line represents a new row of knitting. Every time a coloured-in square is shown, you change colour.

Making up

All the patterns have been designed with the minimum amount of sewing, but there is always some sewing to be done! There are several ways to sew up knitting, so use whichever method you find easiest. Always use the same yarn you knitted with so the stitches are less visible. Darning or tapestry needles with a large eye and blunt end are best so that you don't split the yarn.

Weaving in ends

You will have some loose yarn ends from casting on and binding off, so weave these in first. One of the best ways to weave in the loose ends so they will be invisible is to thread the yarn end through a darning needle and sew it into the seam by passing the needle through the 'bumps' of the stitches on the wrong side of the work. Sew them in for about 1–2in (2.5–5cm) and then snip off any excess yarn.

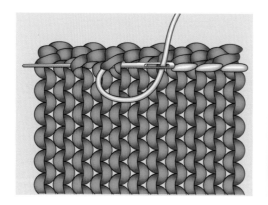

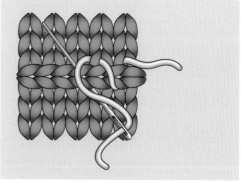

Backstitch (reverse sides out)

Put both knit sides (right sides) together so the wrong sides are facing you. Carefully make small running stitches along the edge, one stitch at a time. Make sure you are sewing in a straight line as close to the edge as possible. It might sound obvious, but it is very easy to pick up stitches that are further away from the edge than you thought. You want the sewing to be as invisible as possible.

Slip stitch (knit sides out)

Put the two pieces of knitting one above the other, knit sides out. Run the thread through the centre of the first stitch on the top piece of knitting then down through the centre of the first stitch on the bottom piece of knitting. Next go through the second stitch on the top piece of knitting and down through the centre of the bottom second stitch. Continue in this way along the row.

Stuffing the toys

Toy stuffing is an essential component for toys. Don't stuff the toys too fully or they will become solid and have no movement. You want the toys to be cuddly. Some of the projects require you to stuff the toys as you go along. This is generally when parts of a toy are long and narrow, such as Mummy and Baby Meerkat. This ensures you distribute an even amount of stuffing throughout the toy.

The stuffing I use is Minicraft Supersoft Toy Stuffing. It comes in bags of 250g (about 9oz) and is made of 100% polyester. If you can't find this particular brand, other suitable brands should be available at haberdashery and craft stores. It is best to use stuffing designed especially for toys so that you can be sure that it is safe for children. Check for the safety logo before you buy it.

I always use my hands to put the stuffing in the toys. You can use your fingers to push the stuffing into small or fiddly pieces.

Sewing in final ends

Once you have stuffed the toy, you will need to close the small opening in the middle of the seam. I knot together the two ends of the yarn used for sewing the seams, then thread the ends through the toy so that the knot is hidden and the ends are kept long. You don't want to cut the ends too short because it makes the knot more likely to come undone.

Finishing touches

One of the best parts about making toys is adding the finishing touches and really bringing the toys to life. It is amazing what adding a pair of beady eyes or a little pink nose can do. Here I've outlined a few techniques for sewing facial features. I also look at adding the little fabric appliqués that some of the toys have, and other little details like crocheted tails and pompoms.

Embroidering details

Spend time making the facial features perfect. It is really effective at making the toys characterful. You can use leftover bits of yarn from previous projects. You can use any sewing stitches to create these features; there really is no rule. You need the stitches to be as firm as possible so that they don't undo and look neat as well. You could use backstitch for the mouth of Monkey Mike, for example, or a single running stitch sewn over and over itself to create the shape of a nose or large eye. You could use a French knot to make the eyes on the smaller toys if you find this easier. Choose what works best for you.

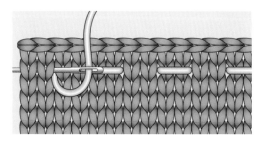

RUNNING STITCH
This is a very simple stitch. Thread a darning or tapestry needle with the yarn you want to use and insert it from the back of the work through to the front where you want the stitch to start. Insert it back through your knitting where you want your stitch to end. This creates an effect like a line of dashes.

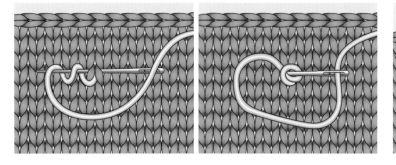

FRENCH KNOT
Bring the needle from the back to the front of the work and wind the yarn twice round the needle. Pull the needle through the twists bringing the yarn through too. This creates the knot. You can twist the yarn round the needle more times if you want a bigger knot and once only for a smaller knot.

BACKSTITCH
Sew a running stitch to create the pattern you want. Once you have reached the end of your pattern go back on yourself, filling in the gaps between the stitches. This should create one single line.

Appliqués

A large number of the projects feature fabric appliqués for the insides of ears or the base of feet. I think this adds a special character to the toys and brings out the nostalgic, personalized nature of the work. You can use cherished pieces of fabric set aside for a special project. Toys provide you with the perfect reason to use such fabrics.

FUSIBLE INTERFACING

Fusible interfacing is perfect for lining your fabric. It stops the edges from fraying and makes the fabric more solid, thereby enabling you to cut out small shapes like the foot pads, ear pads or flower shapes. You can buy fusible interfacing from most haberdashery stores; Vilene is a popular brand.

When using the fusible interfacing, I cut out a piece that is bigger than the template. I then iron this piece onto the fabric and peel off the paper. The interfacing makes the fabric stiffer so it is easier to cut out the shape.

Hold the cut-out piece onto the toy and sew round the edges. If you find it easier, you could pin the cut-out piece to the toy before sewing it on.

SEWING THE FABRIC ON

There are several ways you can sew the fabric details onto the knitting. Try to get your stitching as neat as possible and be creative with the colour of thread you use. The most important thing to ensure is that the fabric is sewn securely to the knitting. Use normal sewing thread rather than knitting yarn.

Rug-making knot

Lenny the Lion's mane is attached with this simple knot.

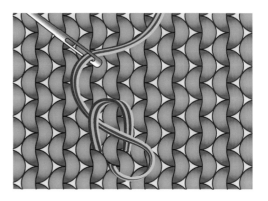

To make each knot, fold a length of yarn, 12in (30cm) long, in half and half again. Using a large tapestry needle, secure all four strands into the stuffed toy close to the guideline. Make one stitch along the guideline, leaving a loop. Bring the needle up again and through the loop created. Pull tight. Continue adding yarn along the guideline until the mane is thick enough. Then trim the mane to the required length.

Crochet chains

Some of the toys feature crocheted chains; Henry Hippo and Zoe the Zebra have crochet-chain tails, while Polly the Parrot has crochet-chain legs. Crocheting a chain is quite simple.

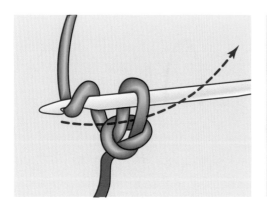

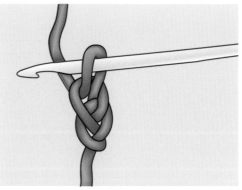

1 Tie a slipknot in the working end of the yarn and place the loop on your crochet hook. Wrap the yarn clockwise over the hook.

2 Pull the yarn through the loop on the hook to form a fresh loop. This is the first chain. Repeat the process until the chain is as long as you want it.

Tassels

Gerry Giraffe and Lenny the Lion have tassels at the end of their tails. These are simply made with an overhand knot in the end of the plait or crochet chain. Cut the yarn ends to make the tassel a pleasing length and unravel the individual strands to give it more body.

Pompoms

Pompoms are used for Ed's hat and Rob the Reindeer's nose. They are very simple to make. You can buy pompom kits that make the process quicker, but here are instructions for the old-fashioned way.

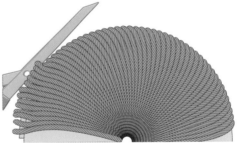

1 Using the template (see Templates), cut out two pieces of card. Remember to cut out the centre hole too. Wrap the yarn in and out of the centre hole, working your way around the pompom ring.

2 Continue wrapping the yarn around the ring until it completely covers all the card. Carefully cut round the edge of the pompom. The two rings of card mean you can slip your scissors between the rings to make cutting easier.

3 Pull the two pieces of card slightly apart and slip a piece of string around the pompom centre. Wrap the string round a few times and knot tightly. It is important to wrap tightly to ensure that the pompom doesn't fall apart. Slip out the pieces of card (cut them if you need to).

Your pompom is complete. Trim round the edge to create a perfectly round ball with no longer tufty bits of yarn.

Templates

MONKEY

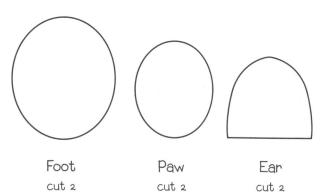

Foot
cut 2

Paw
cut 2

Ear
cut 2

GIRAFFE

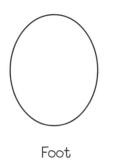

Foot
cut 4

Ear
cut 2

PANDA

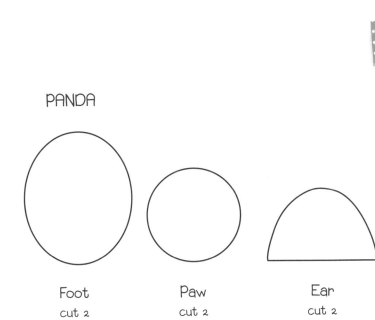

Foot
cut 2

Paw
cut 2

Ear
cut 2

ZEBRA

Foot
cut 4

Ear
cut 2

REINDEER

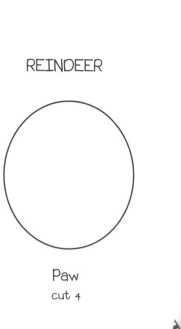

Paw
cut 4

KANGAROOS

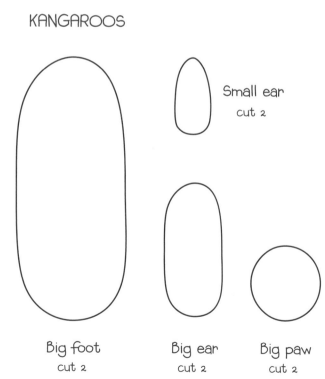

Small ear
cut 2

Big foot
cut 2

Big ear
cut 2

Big paw
cut 2

MEERKATS

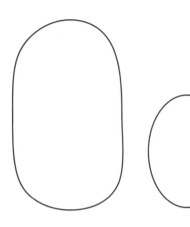

Big foot
cut 2

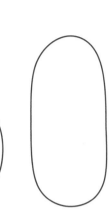

Big hand
cut 2

Small foot
cut 2

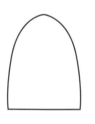

Small hand
cut 2

LION

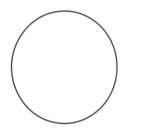

Foot
cut 4

Ear
cut 2

HIPPO

Foot
cut 4

Ear
cut 2

TIGER

Foot
cut 4

POLAR BEAR

Foot
cut 4

Ear
cut 2

Suppliers

Below are some contact details for the suppliers of yarns that I used for making the toys. Many of the toys feature patterned fabrics on their feet and ears. You need small scraps so choose pretty prints from vintage fabrics you have hoarded or from your stash.

ARTESANO
www.artesanoyarns.co.uk
(UK) Artesano Ltd
Unit G, Lamb's Farm Business Park,
Basingstoke Road, Swallowfield
Reading RG7 1PQ
Tel: +44 (0)118 950 3350

CYGNET
www.cygnetyarns.com
Cygnet Yarns Ltd
12-14 Adelaide Street
Bradford
West Yorkshire
BD5 0EF
Tel: +44 (0)1274 743374

HAYFIELD
Supplied by Sirdar, below

MANOS DEL URUGUAY
Supplied by Artesano, above.

PATONS
www.coatscrafts.co.uk
(USA/CAN) 320 Livingstone Avenue South
Listowel, ON, N4W 3H3
Canada
Tel: +1 888 368 8401
www.patonsyarns.com
email: inquire@patonsyarns.com
(UK) Coats Crafts UK
PO Box 22, Lingfield House
Lingfield Point, McMullen Road
Darlington DL1 1YJ
Tel: +44 (0)1325 394237
www.coatscrafts.co.uk
email: consumer.ccuk@coats.com

(AUS) Patons
PO Box 7276, Melbourne Victoria 3004
Tel: +61 (0)3 9380 3888
www.patons.bi3
email: enquiries@auspinners.com.au

ROBIN
Supplied by Twilleys, right.

ROWAN
www.knitrowan.com
(USA) Westminster Fibers Inc
165 Ledge Street, Nashua
New Hampshire 03060
Tel: +1 603 886 5041/5043
www.westminsterfibers.com
email: info@westminsterfibers.com
(UK) Rowan
Green Lane Mill, Holmfirth HD9 2DX
Tel: +44 (0)1484 681881
email: info@knitrowan.com
(AUS) Australian Country Spinners Pty Ltd
Level 7, 409 St Kilda Road
Melbourne, Victoria 3004
Tel: +61 (0)3 9380 3888
email: tkohut@auspinners.com.au

SIRDAR
www.sirdar.co.uk
(USA) Knitting Fever Inc.
315 Bayview Avenue
Amityville, NY 11701
Tel: +1 516 546 3600
www.knittingfever.com
(UK) Sirdar Spinning Ltd
Flanshaw Lane, Alvethorpe
Wakefield WF2 9ND
Tel: +44 (0)1924 371501
email: enquiries@sirdar.co.uk

(AUS) Creative Images
PO Box 106
Hastings, Victoria 3915
Tel: +61 (0)3 5979 1555
email: creative@peninsula.starway.net.au

TWILLEYS
www.twilleys.co.uk
(UK) Twilleys of Stamford
For craft/haberdashery:
Roman Mill, Stamford PE9 1BG
Tel: +44 (0)1780 752661
email: twilleys@tbramsden.co.uk
For head office, administration, handknitting, industrial yarns and shade fringes:
Thomas B. Ramsden (Bradford) Ltd,
Netherfield Road, Guiseley, Leeds
LS20 9PD
Tel: +44 (0)1943 872264
email: sales@tbramsden.co.uk

Yarns used

In the project instructions I have given a generic description of the yarn used for the project so you can easily source a yarn to use or pick something suitable out of your stash. However, if you want to recreate the project exactly, I have specified the yarns used below.

Be warned that yarn companies frequently update their lines, so they may discontinue a certain type of yarn or a certain colour. If the yarns specified below become unavailable, or if you want to use a substitute yarn, you will need to work out how much replacement yarn you need – the meterage or yardage of a ball of yarn can vary considerably between lines and between brands. Make this calculation:
• The number of balls of the recommended yarn x the number of yards/metres per ball = A.
• The number of yards/metres per ball of the substitute yarn = B.
• Divide A by B to calculate the number of balls of substitute yarn required.
Many of the projects use only small amounts of yarn, so you may only need one or two balls of yarn anyway.

ED THE EXPLORER

Rowan Cashsoft DK (merino wool/microfibre/cashmere mix; 142yd (130m) per 1¾oz (50g) ball)
1 ball in colour 540 (**MC**)

Oddments of yarn in deep pink and dark brown

ED'S WARM-WEATHER CLOTHING

The yarn I used for this project was from my stash, but your local yarn supplier should be able to help you find a similar lightweight DK olive green yarn (**A**)

Oddments of yarn in white (**B**), dark brown (**C**) and black

ED'S WINTER WEAR

Rowan Big Wool (merino wool; 87yd (80m) per 3½oz (100g) ball)
1 ball in colour 001 (**MC**)

Oddments of yarn in olive green (**A**) and cream (**B**)

KATH KANGAROO & HER BABY JOEY

The yarn I used for this project was from my stash, but your local yarn supplier should be able to help you find a similar medium-weight Aran light brown yarn (**MC**)

Oddments of yarn in pink, black and white

HENRY HIPPO

Rowan Cashsoft DK (merino wool/microfibre/cashmere mix; 142yd (130m) per 1¾oz (50g) ball)
2 balls in colour 518 (**MC**)

Oddments of yarn in pink (**A**), white and dark brown

POLLY THE PARROT

Robin DK (acrylic; 329yd (300m) per 3½oz (100g) ball)
1 ball in each of colours 018 (**MC**) and 286 (**A**)

Patons Fairytale Colour 4 Me DK (100% wool; 98yd (90m) per 1¾oz (50g) ball)
1 ball in colour 4957 (**B**)
Oddments of DK yarn in cream (**C**) and black

MONKEY MIKE

Artesano Aran (wool/alpaca mix; 144yd (132m)
per 3½oz (100g) skein)
1 skein in each of colours C854 (**MC**) and
CA03 (**A**)

Oddment of yarn in dark brown

TIMOTHY TIGER

Manos del Uruguay Silk Blend Multicoloured
(merino wool /silk mix; 295yd (270m) per 3½oz
(100g) skein)
1 skein in colour 6610 (**MC**)

Rowan Cashsoft DK (merino wool/microfibre/
cashmere mix; 142yd (130m) per 1¾oz (50g) ball)
1 ball in black (**A**)

Rowan Cashsoft DK (merino wool/microfibre/
cashmere mix; 142yd (130m) per 1¾oz (50g) ball)
1 ball in white (**B**)

PENNY THE PANDA

The yarn I used for this project was from my stash,
but your local yarn supplier should be able to help
you find similar lightweight DK black (**A**) and white
(**B**) yarn

MUMMY & BABY MEERKAT

Hayfield Bonus DK (100% acrylic; 307yd (280m)
per 3 ½ oz (100g) ball)
1 ball of colour 964 (**MC**)

Oddments of yarn in black (**A**) and white

GERRY GIRAFFE

Rowan Felted Tweed DK (merino/alpaca/viscose
mix; 191yd (175m) per 1¾oz (50g) ball)
1 ball of each of colours 160 (**MC**) and 175 (**A**)

Oddment of yarn in dark brown

LENNY THE LION

Manos del Uruguay Silk Blend Multicoloured
(merino wool/silk mix; 295yd (270m) per 3½oz
(100g) skein)
1 skein in colour 6610 (**MC**)

Rowan Cocoon (merino wool/kid mohair mix;
126yd (115m) per 3½oz (100g) ball)
1 ball in colour 815 (**A**)

Oddments of DK yarn in white and black

ZOE THE ZEBRA

Rowan Pure Wool DK (100% wool: 137yd
(125m) per 1¾oz (50g) ball)
1 ball in each of black (**MC**) and white (**A**)

PATSY POLAR BEAR

Cygnet Superwash DK (100% wool; 114yd
(104m) per 1¾oz (50g) ball)
1 ball in colour 2195 (**MC**)

Oddment of yarn in black

ROB THE REINDEER

Twilleys Freedom Purity (wool/alpaca mix 79yd
(72m) per 1¾oz (50g) ball)
2 balls in colour 782 (**MC**)

Cygnet Superwash DK (100% wool; 114yd
(104m) per 1¾oz (50g) ball)
1 ball in colour 4315 (**A**)

Oddments of yarn in green, red, yellow, black
and white

About the author

Laura Long graduated in 2003 with a First Class knitted textiles degree from Central St. Martins College of Art and Design. Since then she has been working out of her central London studio designing, making and selling her knitted creations to boutiques and galleries all over the world.

Teaching and freelance work has played an important part in her business. She designs, makes and creates patterns and pieces for designers, knitting magazines and pattern books, and her clients have included Rowan yarns, *Simply Knitting* and *Knit Today* magazines, and publications such as *Collective Knitting* and *Holiday Knits*. She has also taught both machine and hand knitting to people of all ages at Loop and the Cockpit Arts.

Dolls, fairytales and fantasy played an important part in Laura's childhood – a childhood full of happy, everlasting memories. It is for this reason that she has developed a collection of childhood characters, knitted creatures and dolls with personalities all of their own.

Acknowledgments

Thanks to Katy and everyone at David & Charles for your patience and support, and for allowing me to write another toy book. Thank you also to my studio friends Katie and Zoe for putting up with my dreadful singing and endless cheesy music while I knit and to Will for helping with the map. But most importantly:

THANK YOU MUM. Without you, I could never have written this book.

Index

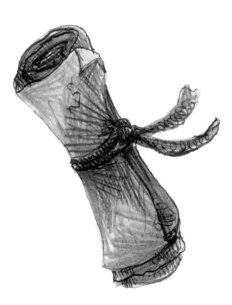

A DAVID & CHARLES BOOK
© F&W Media International, LTD 2012

David & Charles is an imprint of F&W Media International, LTD
Brunel House, Forde Close, Newton Abbot, TQ12 4PU, UK

F&W Media International, LTD is a subsidiary of F+W Media, Inc.
4700 East Galbraith Road, Cincinnati, OH 45236

First published in the UK and USA in 2012
Digital edition published in 2012

Text and designs © Laura Long 2012
Layout and photography © F&W Media International, LTD 2012

A catalogue record for this book is available from the British Library.

ISBN-13: 978-1-4463-0146-3 paperback
ISBN-10: 1-4463-0146-X paperback

ISBN-13: 978-1-4463-5575-6 e-pub
ISBN-10: 1-4463-5575-6 e-pub

ISBN-13: 978-1-4463-5574-9 PDF
ISBN-10: 1-4463-5574-8 PDF

Paperback edition printed in China by RR Donnelley
for F&W Media International LTD,
Brunel House, Forde Close, Newton Abbot, TQ12 4PU, UK

10 9 8 7 6 5 4 3 2 1

Publisher Alison Myer
Acquisitions Editor Katy Denny
Desk Editor Jeni Hennah
Project Editors Karen Hemingway and Anna Southgate
Art Editor Charly Bailey
Senior Designer Victoria Marks
Photographer Lorna Yabsley
Senior Production Controller Kelly Smith

The Publisher would like to thank Plant World Gardens & Nursery, Newton Abbot for allowing
photography to be taken in their 'Gardens of the World': www.plant-world-seeds.com

F+W Media, Inc. publishes high quality books on a wide range
of subjects. For more great book ideas visit: www.rucraft.co.uk